Fr. Benedict Groeschel, CFR

Faithful Son of the Church	3
Loving Father of the Poor	27
Ardent Preacher of the Gospel	41
Dedicated Follower of St. Francis	53
Conclusion	63
Footnotes	67
Sources	69

There are some people in this world that just seem to "get" it. This phrase might seem a bit cliché or trite. Yet it becomes clear to those who experience this type of person that a close connection with the Creator and fresh perspective on life are the keys to this holy kind of contentment. Fr. Groeschel is one of these people. Those who knew him personally, or knew of him, or who experienced him through his publications or talks could see this. His outlook was genuine and his devotion to the Lord sincere. Blossoming from these things was an inspirational man who emanated the radiance of God's favor.

Fr. Groeschel was described in his EWTN tribute as a "faithful son of the Church, loving father of the poor, ardent preacher of the gospel, and dedicated follower of St. Francis." While it is difficult to summarize a man such as Fr. Groeschel into a few short phrases, these will serve as a focal point to this exploration into his life, works, and legacy. Whenever possible, his own words will be used to exemplify these aspects as his prolific writing and talks provide ample evidence. As a TV host, we are blessed with quite a lot of footage of this man and his mind. With over thirty books written as well, there is not much left to say about that man that he has not already said himself. I have chosen two of these works specifically for a myriad of reasons. *Arise From Darkness: What to Do when Life Doesn't Make Sense* is a sort of manual for those dealing with anxiety, fear, hopelessness, death, addiction, or other kinds of darkness that threaten one's faith life or personal life. It was written to provide some solace in the hope of gaining God's grace and a bit of understanding. Much like the other book used frequently throughout this work, it has a deeply psychological aspect that showcases Fr. Groeschel's deep knowledge of the human mind and how faith can offer help to those suffering mentally and spiritually. The other work, *Stumbling Blocks or Stepping Stones: Spiritual Answers to Psychological Questions* is similar in this aspect. It is different in that it focuses more deeply on the Scriptures and other Christian literature for guidance in the area of psychology. These and video clips from the EWTN television show Sunday Night Live serve as the main sources for the look into Fr. Benedict Groeschel's life, mind, and ministry. Accounts of those who knew him or worked with him are also included as needed to round out the man we are attempting to investigate. If the four areas already mentioned were not able to cover all that Fr. Groeschel was, looking into his work as a speaker and writer as well as his psychological insights would likely be more than enough to flesh out the man we are attempting to remember.

To start, though, one usually turns to the beginning. The caring and witty man hosting *Sunday Night Prime* was not always white haired. There was indeed a time when he was a fourth-grade paper boy, working diligently to manage his sixty plus paper route. While he was born Robert Peter Groeschel, it seems that even his early life hinted at his future life of even more hard work, service, and holiness under his later adopted name of Benedict.[1] His education was precisely what one would expect- fully Catholic from start to finish, heralding Immaculate Conception High School of Montclair, New Jersey as his alma mater. After this, Groeschel entered St. Francis Friary in Huntington, Indiana. His novitiate was completed in Detroit and he took his temporary vows in 1952, taking the religious name of Benedict Joseph after

Saint Benedict Joseph Labre, patron saint of the homeless. His journey in education did not stop when he took these vows, though, nor did his spiritual one. Fr. Benedict Groeschel would go on to earn a master's degree from Iona College and merit a doctorate of education with an emphasis in psychology from the prestigious Columbia University[2]. Though highly educated, Fr. Groeschel never failed to remain approachable, kind, and humorous. He even went so far in one of his speeches as to jokingly discourage youths from pursuing a degree in Psychology as he had to endure thirty-one years of schooling (quite the unappealing prospect to a group of youngsters and teens)[3]. As for Fr. Groeschel's other abundant career, religious, and life highlights and milestones, we shall encounter them under the four defining features that were previously named, that is, that he was a faithful son of the Church and remained committed to it even when it was not the easy thing to do; that he was a loving father of the poor and gave most of his life to the service of others; that he was an ardent preacher of the gospel in that he was both a knowledgeable and a gifted orator as well as a prolific writer; and lastly that he was a dedicated follower of St. Francis and a great champion of religious life and orders as well as the saints. Through these four pillars we will hopefully be able to construct the whole of Fr. Benedict Groeschel and the significant impact that he made while he was with us here in this life.

Faithful Son of the Church

It is an understatement to say that society does not always favor Christians. Catholics especially seem to get a majority of the criticisms in our modern times and bear the brunt of most of society's attacks on religion. Fr. Benedict Groeschel was an amazing example of what Matthew chapter five verse ten states, "Blessed are those who have been persecuted for the sake of righteousness, for theirs is the kingdom of heaven."[4] Keeping the faith amidst the temptations and troubles of the secular world is one thing. It is a completely different struggle one endures when one remains faithful to the Church but must oppose those who also under the umbrella of the Mother Church, too. This is a unique kind of battle and one that is becoming more and more prevalent with so many different voices and cultures participating in the discussion of what it means to be Catholic and what the best practices are to express this. In the words of Fr. Groeschel,

> I was almost a priest fifty years and I watched the Church get into trouble. When I was a kid, when I was a young priest, we didn't have trouble, but 1968 was a very, very bad year. There were revolutions everywhere...things really started to deteriorate. Public morality, the control of media by moral principles, disappeared. The movies in U.S. are anti-Catholic movies and they especially hate Catholic priests... Hollywood mocks everything; it's a society of mockery... [yet] I got thrown out of four seminaries for being a faith catholic favorable to the Pope. They were crazy times, there were scandals, many priests left...orders have fallen apart. Things were spiraling down...many of you had not-so-good religious educations...what are you? I could bring people in here who work actually for the church that would be disappointed to meet you. You're too Catholic, too religious, too Christian. They want to have the Church be one big happy family of nudniks... so why are you here? It is the *work of the Holy Spirit*. [5]

Where others might conjure up excuses because of their hardships and trials and use these as reason to stray from the Church, Fr. Groeschel did not. In fact, in his message on Divine Mercy, Fr. Groeschel spoke that it is a sad but true fact that tragedy can happen at any moment. It is belief in the mercy of God that allows us to come out of that bad situation better off from having experienced it. Even death, which looks exteriorly to most as an evil or "bad" might truly be a blessing. To those who would abandon the mother Church for such reasons, Groeschel has little but criticism. Those who leave the faith and turn instead to secular culture are turning towards "garbage", as Fr. Groeschel would define it. He would be the first man to tell you that the current state of society at large was destitute, immoral, and "trash". In an episode of *Sunday Night Live* with Archbishop Dolan, Fr. Groeschel and he discuss that the Church is not merely under attack by our current culture of death and permissiveness. *The New York Times* in particular was subject to a great deal of criticism from these two religious men for its (seemingly) purposeful crusade against the Holy Catholic Church. While criticism is often necessary to keep organizations in line, the attacks on the Church by the media lack the fairness and balance needed to make the reviews constructive. While there are many people and media sources that are at peace with (or ambivalent towards) the Church, there are others that are militant in their hate towards the it, a phenomenon that Bishop Dolan attributes to the rise in popularity of this "chic" and modern Atheism. Because it is the new and popular point of view, many are jumping on this bandwagon of hate towards religion in a broad sense. Religious extremists are no positive force, either, however, and are more in line with the extreme non-believers in the spectrum of belief. They give a poor example of what it means to be a loving follower of Christ, as their hardline views often lack forgiveness and understanding. Fr. Benedict and Bishop Nolan also remind the viewers that the Church is also under actual attack in some Islamic and Asian countries, where Catholics are physically persecuted for their beliefs and dedication to the faith.

Back here in the United States, the shift away from moral values and family life was particularly interesting to Groeschel especially considering his extended background in the field of psychology. Cultural trends that pointed to increased selfishness and the desire to find pleasure and quickly acquire possessions quickly were at the top of Fr. Benedict's criticisms. That said, he was never one to shy away from condemning the current state of affairs within Mother Church as well. He noted that many of us failed to see the trouble that the Church has gotten into in recent decades because of the severity of the cultural problems; we Catholics were blinded by the comparison and failed to see the slip in orthodoxy that had been occurring since the Second Vatican Council.

In his written introduction to the Catholic Directory of Authentically Catholic Colleges, Groeschel notes that the list is quite short. The level of apostasy within the majority of Catholic colleges here in the United States troubled Groeschel very deeply and he spoke out against their false or watered-down teachings frequently. Yet, he remained persistent. Instead of dismissing these institutions, he makes an important point in this particular talk. He states that these schools are just like any other consumer good: as we experience an upward trend in orthodoxy, the faithful schools will flourish as they will be in higher demand. Those that accept and participate in this backwards culture of ours will be left to either change to compete within the market, or be completely abandoned and left behind. Always tempering his criticisms with humor and kindness, Groeschel lessens the blow of his harsh critique with some sound advice to the colleges soon to be among those left behind: do some housecleaning and get rid of the problems that are holding you back from making this list of Authentically Catholic Colleges.

While Groeschel was always a devoted son of the Church, his love was like that of any parent (and even like that of the Mother Church, herself). Any good parent knows that scolding your child might be the best thing for them and is a lesser evil that contributes to a future good (i.e. their happiness, wellbeing, or health). Such was Fr. Groeschel's devotion to the Church. He nearly always backed the position of the Holy Father (regardless of the subject) and was quick to dismiss things like "cafeteria Catholicism" in which people pick and choose the part of the faith they want to remain faithful towards. Groeschel never bowed down in the face of the trends that circulated within Catholicism. He chose instead to remain adherent to all of the Church's core values and principles. He did this is such a way that allowed him to remain very kind, loving and forgiving. A great example of this is evidenced in his discussion on same sex marriage on an episode of his EWTN show, *Sunday Night Prime*. Instead of condemning homosexuals as sinners and dismissing them completely, Groeschel takes a position that does not single them out in particular. He takes the side that the Catholic Church is "against anything that cheapens marriage". He discusses with his guest on the show that the Church is pro-civil rights, pro-marriage, not anti-gay. They point out that those not in a married relationship must remain chaste regardless of their sexual orientation. Pornography is condemned by the church because of its tendency to corrupt the mind and dignity of the human person. Even those who are divorced in the church are required to go through the process of annulment if they wish to date or enter into another relationship. They are not allowed communion if they do so without seeking this annulment first. Catholics are in the business of protecting the family and society. Even Harvard studies showed that when the traditional family unit broke down, poverty and violence greatly increased. Groeschel and his co-host also noted that natural law predates the Bible and history itself and it is unwise to go against the current if one wishes to preserve one's life.

With all of this said, Groeschel was adamant that the Catholic Church does not hate gays. He spoke about the options that are out there for homosexuals within the faith, i.e. living a chaste life and remaining in communion with the Mother Church. He also remained amazingly hopeful that with the intercession of the Holy Spirit, the Church would experience a counter-reaction to combat acceptance of this new-aged thinking in which people are fighting for homosexual marriage. Even taking a (some could say) unpopular or unfavorable side of the issue on the legalization of gay marriage and the role of gays within the Catholic Church, Groeschel remained extremely hopeful that things would improve and the Church would be listened to. He also, as stated before, took up this position with a heart of sincere love and encouragement for homosexuals. He was never unkind or uncaring. He remained true to the teaching of the Church on a hard-line issue and was able to emphasize the love and forgiveness that the Church offers, all while staying true to his position. Instead of bowing down to what many "modern" thinkers within the Catholic Church are teaching, Fr. Groeschel backed the official doctrine of the Faith, even if it made him seem callous or decreased his popularity. He was a man of strong conviction and dedication to the teachings of the Holy Catholic Church as well as the writings of our Holy Fathers.

Concerning this positive change towards increased orthodoxy, there were many reasons Fr. Benedict gave us that encouraged the aforementioned hopefulness. While he had great respect for the Popes of recent history, he knew that no one person can run the church. The contact point between the Church and the faithful is with the priest. While the seminaries failed to make strong priests to guide the faithful through the sexual revolution and post Vatican II era, young men are now getter better educations and faith formation that they previously were, in the opinion of Fr. Benedict. Instead of rejecting Humane Vitae and accepting many of secular society's ideas of permissiveness, young priests are going back to the more orthodox roots of the faith. Unfortunately, many of those in higher positions remain from the era of poor formation and misdirection. Currently, however, we are beginning to see better appointments and a realization that strong men are needed for the priesthood and the higher positions of power like that of the Bishops and Cardinals. Fr. Benedict felt that the Pope was able to work from the top down by making better appointments just as the seminaries could work from the bottom up to build a foundation of priests that will support the faith through the next century.[6]

Even with these changes, it is not always easy to remain faithful to the teachings of the Church, especially when we are in a society of "garbage". We are constantly bombarded with others telling us that kindness and mercy means complete acceptance and permissiveness of things like same-sex marriage, abortion, and pre-marital sex. Groeschel was able to remain very orthodox while maintaining a completely open heart for everyone. He was ever hopeful as well. He was sure to celebrate anyone who joined the Church, especially after living a life of Agnosticism or Atheism, and continually prayed for those who had been members of the faith but had left the community of faithful. He just knew in his heart that the youth of the Pope John Paul II and Pope Benedict XVI generations were going to turn the faith around and that there would be a large counter shift in both the Church and Society. This hope was never false bravado, but a genuine belief that the Holy Spirit would come down and work through the youth and young adults to turn the Mother Church around. He was never discouraged by the state of things. He never lost faith in the truth of the orthodoxy of the Roman Catholic Church. In this, one could argue that he most showed his fidelity to the Church. Closely behind this, or perhaps tied, was Groeschel's commitment to the position of Holy Father. Groeschel spoke very highly of Pope John Paul II and Pope Benedict XVI and respected and admired their work. He hardly mentioned John Paul II without saying he expected full canonization and would claim that he thought that Benedict XVI would soon be behind him. He spoke highly of them both as writers, religious, and leaders, and was largely in agreement with their decisions and writings. If Fr. Groeschel had a serious grievance with either of those two Popes, it is impossible to find in the myriad of archives, writings, and videos of the priest.

In a particular episode of *Sunday Night Prime*, Fr. Benedict Groeschel speaks of Pope Benedict XVI most fondly. He claims that the Pope had "a brain and three-quarters", praising him for his amazing scholarly work. He was joyed that even after his appointment, Pope Benedict still had the time to continue his writing and pursue his scholastic endeavors. He spoke of how gentle and kind he was; while many expected him to be harsh and unforgiving considering the position he rose from (reminding many of the terrible Inquisitions of the Church's past history), Benedict was a fair and loving Pope. He exemplified a great humility and was reportedly very easy to talk to. He is also known for being a great teacher and writer. His aforementioned approachability seeps into his writing; instead of reading as pontifical or didactic, his works are often less formal than one would expect and very applicable to common lives. He does not shy away from the hard questions, either, or dance around difficult issues. He asks these challenging questions in his writings and supplies well informed answers. In his book, *Jesus of Nazareth*, he effectively takes on the accusations of those involved in the Jesus Seminar[7] and works to reverse the damage done by this modern obsession with discovering the "historical Jesus". Fr. Groeschel candidly agrees with Pope Benedict on the matter. Both men emphasize that Jesus is here, now, and clearly present today in the Church and in our lives. Instead of digging up bits of ancient history, both Pope Benedict and Fr. Benedict emphasize that we should seek out a personal relationship with Him. Neither Pope Benedict nor Fr. Groeschel was dismissive of history, though. Instead, Pope Benedict speaks with great reverence for the Jewish people and the Old Testament. He reminds the faithful that it is crucially important to view Jesus through the historical lens provided by the Judaism of the Old Testament. Through *this* cultural background, one is able to better grasp who Jesus was and what His motivations were. The work of those from the Jesus Seminar is largely unnecessary. These papal writings such as Pope Benedict's book *Jesus of Nazareth* are helping to educate the youth and refute the problematic works of those who deny Christ's divinity. While the colleges will likely be the last to change, we are again reminded that Fr. Groeschel was so full of hope for the future of the youth and the Catholic Church as a whole.

While it is hard to navigate the line between love of the Church and the desire for reform, Fr. Groeschel did it well. This last point – that he was ever hopeful- kept him from becoming too harsh or jaded. He spoke often of the change among the youth towards orthodoxy. He believed that they were more serious about their faith than previous generations and that it was in spite of the elders in the church that the youth were leaning this way. Many of the younger Catholic families have gone back to having more children, to homeschooling, and raising children with a more devout view of the Church. Even with the decline in religious sisters in the Catholic school systems, there are other, new opportunities for the youth that are developing. For instance, there was collaboration with youth and religious to produce *Youcat*, a youth-oriented Catechism that offers an abridged, relevant guide to the faith. In the introduction, Pope Benedict writes in the introduction that it is designed to deepen the faith of the young adults so that it will be more deeply rooted than the previous generations. Fr. Groeschel knew also what Pope Benedict did: that the future of the church was truly left to the younger generation. With this said, neither man was deluded that this would happen overnight or was a sure thing. Whereas Pope John Paul II was often criticized for his rosy view of the future of the Church, Pope Benedict and Fr. Groeschel both worked towards and hoped to achieve short term, realistic goals. However, the devotion to Catholic authenticity and this idea of reform was found among the Popes that preceded Pope John Paul II and set the stage for him and Pope Benedict XVI to do more amazing work[8]. Fr. Groeschel also defended Pope Benedict from the ridiculous claim that he was an anti-Semite. As mentioned, Pope Benedict had a great reverence for the Jews and the Old

Testament. As expressed in his book, *Jesus of Nazareth*, Pope Benedict believed that the Jews had an important purpose. Just as Christians saw Jesus as the New Law (and looked to the Gospels after He ascended into heaven), the Jews had to shift their focus from the Temple (after it was destroyed) to a more scripturally based faith, too. The Jews were not rendered obsolete by the destruction of their Temple or the coming of Christ. Rather, they too had a new way of approaching their faith with their focus now on the Torah.

While the Catholic Church is responsible historically for some anti-Semitism, this is not representative of the whole of the faith or the Pope in particular. Fr. Groeschel also addresses this. He begins by reminding his audience that the Church is a human and a flawed institution. However, it is often misunderstood, too. Pope Benedict give an example of this by using the famous "blood curse" that Jesus spoke during his Passion, cursing those who did this to Him and their children as well. In no way did this mean that Jesus cursed all of the Jews. Rather, he cursed the temple aristocracy that was utterly corrupt; He cursed the crowd that condemned Him instead of Barabbas. He did not blame the whole of the Jews for this. In fact, His followers, His friends, and His mother were all still practicing Jews at this time. The Pope points out in his book that the blood of Jesus has redemptive qualities and should not be considered a curse in any situation. Throughout His ministry, Jesus accepted naysayers and enemies with love and patience. The Church continues to do so and Fr. Benedict Groeschel is one to remind the faithful that the recent Popes have done a great job of defending the faith and helping it stay on the true path.

With all of that said, Fr. Benedict was not one to go along with just anything that the Church said and voiced that there was still great need for change. He quite vocally disagreed with the historical banning of the devotion of the Divine Mercy and was quite glad that it was reinstated. He also speaks of the many mistakes of past Church councils, leaders within the Faith, and other members of the church without reservation and often with much disapproval.

Fr. Benedict did not sugar coat his message to the faithful, either. In a piece about prayer, specifically that of praise and thanksgiving, Fr. Benedict Groeschel condemned those Christians who only pray when they have great need of God. While prayers of intercession certainly have their place, seeking God only in these times limits one's spiritual growth and does not allow for a richer spiritual life in general. He critiqued the faithful for not participating more in the other forms of prayer, such as adoration, thanksgiving, contrition, and contemplative prayer. He specifically encouraged an increase in prayers of adoration and thanksgiving. Fr. Benedict stated that this is how one can change an ordinary life to an interesting one that is full of joy. He claimed also that it is part of our natural, human relationship with God. Thanksgiving is also known for being part of almost every religion's repertoire. Those who participate in this prayer will have an increase in devotion, reverence, attention, and prayerfulness in general. Showing again his great reverence, love, and knowledge of Scripture, Fr. Groeschel reminds the faithful that the Psalms are a great place to start with this. He mentions Psalm Ninety-Five in particular, quoting:

> Come, let us sing for joy to the Lord;
>> let us shout aloud to the Rock of our salvation.
> 2 Let us come before him with thanksgiving
>> and extol him with music and song.
> 3 For the Lord is the great God,
>> the great King above all gods.
> 4 In his hand are the depths of the earth,
>> and the mountain peaks belong to him.
> 5 The sea is his, for he made it,
>> and his hands formed the dry land.
> 6 Come, let us bow down in worship,
>> let us kneel before the Lord our Maker;
> 7 for he is our God
>> and we are the people of his pasture,

the flock under his care.

Today, if only you would hear his voice,

8 "Do not harden your hearts as you did at Meribah, [a]

as you did that day at Massah[b] in the wilderness,

9 where your ancestors tested me;

they tried me, though they had seen what I did.

10 For forty years I was angry with that generation;

I said, 'They are a people whose hearts go astray,

and they have not known my ways.'

11 So I declared on oath in my anger,

'They shall never enter my rest.'"

Fr. Benedict said that he read this Psalm every day as a reminder of the importance of adoring God. He said there were so many different ways to pursue this type of prayer, though, and did not limit himself or others to just this Psalm or the Psalms in general. Another obvious type of adoration is that of Eucharistic Adoration. A not so obvious way is by looking at the sky and pondering the beautiful aspects of God's creation. Through this form of prayer, Christians are able to admire the greatness and immensity of God and His creation in a way that subtly reminds us of our humility as well. God made all of it; when we stop to proverbially "smell the roses", we are able to take a short break from the regularity of ordinary everyday life and escape into something grander than ourselves. One will never again be bored because they will have a greater and more regular awareness of the greatness and presence of God. Fr. Groeschel even looked to the city for inspiration for prayers of adoration. He humorously pointed to the New York subway system as a metaphor of the Last Judgment (certainly an awe-inspiring event, and a rather dark and dirty one, too). All of these opportunities are there for us to ponder and adore God's glory and greatness. Once we are in the habit of doing so, life becomes so much richer and more meaningful than if we do not participate in prayers of adoration. Even while in prison, Fr. Benedict meditated on God's awesome powers and this brought him comfort and joy in the midst of an unpleasant situation.

When one spends more time in adoration, one also learns of the mysteries of God. So often, the aspects of life we fail to understand are what being us pain, sadness, and confusion. When one spends time in adoration of God, the mysterious becomes less frightening. One is more prepared for the mysterious, the unexpected, and the unplanned parts of life that would normally give on a great deal of anxiety and hurt. As Fr. Benedict said, "You get that you won't get it". In this way, the one who sends time in adoration is ready to accept life's surprises and handle and move on from the unpleasant ones[9].

Fr. Benedict (as one well-schooled in the area of psychology) understood that these hardships in life are often the cause of defection from the Church. By encouraging adoration, Fr. Benedict ensured that he and others would handle these problems better and remain within the Catholic community. He was not just faithful to the Church himself; he encouraged others to remain faithful as well and in this way worked to grow the faith community. His book *Stumbling Blocks or Stepping Stones: Spiritual Answers to Psychological Questions* offers many examples of this. The introduction cuts right to the heart of one of the biggest problems among the faithful, that is, pride. Fr. Benedict, in an attempt to combat infidelity to the Church and the Gospel message writes:

> The pretense that one is a really good Christian in spite of innumerable warnings in the Gospels and Epistles against such illusory thinking is simply a version of the general denial on the part of the human race that has caused so many cultures and individuals to avoid casting a critical eye on how they act.[10]

Fr. Benedict knew so much about the faith and a large part of how he demonstrated that he was faithful to the Church was encouraging proper devotion. He wrote many books and spoke frequently about how a proper prayer life was paramount to having a good relationship to Christ and the Church. There are so many different forms and varieties in which to participate; Fr. Benedict, while orthodox, did not look with disdain on the Charismatic movement within the Church and regarded most varieties of devotion equally. By supporting proper prayer and worship so frequently and vocally, Fr. Benedict helped others remain faithful sons and daughters of the Church as well.

Also in the same vein, Fr. Benedict warned against "fallen-angelism" and types of narcissism that had become popular at the end of the twentieth century and other common fallacies or spiritual traps that people often fall into. He wrote, "You may be focusing all of your attention on avoiding obvious sins when you should be reorganizing your life so as to function in a more human and responsible way, that is to say, in a more Christian way." Throughout his book *Stumbling Blocks and Stepping Stones*, Fr. Benedict continually looks for ways to help the faith remain present and active within the Church (like avoiding these pitfalls), instead of falling away when they encounter real strife, hardship, confusion, or doubt. He emphasizes frequently the need to look for ways not to get rid of sin completely, but to use it against itself and help on grow in the faith.

He also continuously looks towards Scripture and Tradition to help him in this endeavor and recommends that the other faithful do the same. For example, he reminds his readers that the old catechism has not changed and that the outline for what constitutes a mortal sin has not wavered. Not one to be totally stuck in the past, Fr. Benedict goes on to allow that modern studied in Psychology and other scientific areas have allowed us to better understand the conditions of the mind and what exactly "full consent" means. In this way, Fr. Benedict showed that he was always looking to help inform the faithful about the Church and her teachings and keep the message while also accepting modern advancements that supported this.[11]

Concerning the history of the Church, Fr. Groeschel was not blinded by his love for the Faith. He still remained humorous in the many foibles of the Church through the ages and was quick to dismiss the Church's past mistakes. He was not so blinded with love for the faith that he did not ever question it. Rather, he considered questions of faith with the great love and tenderness. That said, Groeschel admitted that we lived through the pontificate of one of the Greatest Popes (Pope John Paul II) because he had had such a great effect on secular society. However, Fr. Groeschel calls him out for being too kind for those disloyal to the Church and that these unfaithful members therefore missed out on possible conversion of heart. Reform must begin in the heart for it to be effective and Fr. Groeschel was bracingly honest about how exactly he felt that reform should occur. His love was just like that of a loving parent. While some might call him harsh, any critique he had of the faith was born of true love and desire for what is best for the faith. He writes, "I love the Church and can't pretend to love only the heavenly Church while ignoring or disdaining the Church on Earth. But often I get angry at the Church, or rather some segment of it. I've supported the Church when there were things going on with which I deeply disagreed. I suspect we all have...[12]"

Fr. Groeschel did speak about the great need of reform both within the Church and society. The need for renewal and reform was apparent to him. Christianity as a whole also needed reform according to Fr. Groeschel, as did the United States as a whole: "No nation survives which kills its own children[13]". The media is terrible and shies from the truth but the clergy say nothing. So how does one go about reforming a whole society and faith? One has to avoid progressivism and the tendency or urge to lean towards archaic ideals equally. With all of this in mind, Groeschel championed the Church even though we face behemoths like MTV, which have so much money that it is nearly impossible to fight their message of moral depravity[14]. He also wrote about the kind of secular opinion that causes lack of belief in the teachings of the Church. Religious freedom, he states, has caused a certain blasé attitude that treats religion as recreation. Not one to think of the Church as blameless, Fr. Groeschel also condemns those members of the Church that have acquired financial wealth. One is justified in regarding members of the Church who live well off of the funds of the Church with suspicion. Just as culpable are those who are especially self-righteous, those who are intellectually detached, and those with immature personal faith lives.[15] Also included in this litany of causes of unbelief are the highly intellectual. When prides comes as a result of this intellect, this arrogance can very easily lead one from the Church, often taking others away as well. St. Paul warns of this when he writes to the highly educated and "progressive" Corinthians.[16] The history of the Church is riddled with incidents of this kind of intellectual pride separating people from Christ, starting with some of the very first followers. As Fr. Groeschel explains, "brilliant minds can be caught in a limited perspective or dominated by a particular technique or point of view that seems to contain the whole answer. This can plunge the thinker into a bottomless pit of his own doubts. Then, if pride or vanity which are common enough vices for us all, take hold of his thinking, his gifts of intelligence can easily be dominated by arrogance."[17] Sadly, it is those who are great thinkers that are capable of being greatly corrupted and poisoning others against the Faith in addition to their own defection. To combat this, Fr. Groeschel wrote that humility is the answer. Understanding that the human mind is simply not capable of understanding everything and that true wisdom is gained by realizing how much one does not understand are crucial to avoiding this common enemy of the Faith. The Church is always suffering attacks from within and without, according to Fr. Groeschel and the faithful must constantly be on guard against them.

Such a large part of being a faithful son of the Church was also wrapped up in Fr. Groeschel's work as a counselor to priests and laity alike, as well as to the poor. Understanding the psychological impacts of people's faith issues allowed him to offer solace, advice, and good counsel to those he spoke with. He helped so many others remain faithful, come back to Mother Church, and even convert. It is no surprise that he encountered many who had undergone hardship in their lives and needed his words. In the current climate within our Western Culture, he was right to speak out about these problems.

Another large problem that brought so many away from the Church that Fr. Benedict wrote about in particular was this sadly common issue of having anger at God. In a very poignant way, Fr. Groeschel attacks those who use this excuse and the culture that permits it, saying, "Perhaps you are angry at God because your view of Him is too narrow. You may have thought He was a genie, a magical being who manipulates your life to suit you pleasure. Perhaps you never really believed that the cross is the lot of every Christian, and now you are faced with it and cannot escape it. Those who deny the inescapable reality of suffering are prone to bitter despair when it eventually comes their way.[18]" The world and secular culture are constantly telling us that we deserve to be happy, that we are to seek happiness wherever we want it, that suffering is unjust and does not happen to us in our protected bubble of the First World. Tragedy, in truth, can strike anyone at any time which Fr. Groeschel gently reminds us. It is no wonder that the dialogue of self-fulfillment and "make-your-own" happiness has contributed to those leaving the Faith and lowered the level of religiosity and devotion in general. When the expectations are set so high, even the slightest set back can shake one's faith and perceptions of God to the point of total disbelief. Additionally, the happiness that people are promised in society is rooted in material goods and physical pleasures. With such a fickle basis of happiness, it is no wonder that there is this move away from Christianity and faith. Also, to be considered is that the principles of happiness are defined by secular society and are the measuring stick by which spiritual happiness is measured. Neither Christianity nor any reputable faith claims to make life perfect and happy. Fr. Benedict wisely addresses this, "We should not pretend that any religion, including Christianity, removes dread from life...the foundation of dread is the fear that all we have and all we are will be lost, and that we will pass into oblivion...this is not an idle fear...almost all human beings hope that death is not the end. I think life would become impossible if we were without the hope of life after death."[19] Indeed, the hope of the afterlife is often what allows us Christians to continue on in this valley of tears.

Benedict Groeschel also spoke in particular about how society had really gone wrong concerning the Christmas season. Fr. Benedict had made an entire video on just the proper preparation for the Advent season. He speaks about the terrible commercialization of the Christmas holiday and how so little of the Advent season is about Christ. He compares it to his time in grammar school, in which the small children saved money for the poor, were reminded of the many opportunities to be generous with stories like "A Christmas Carol", and sang meaningful Christmas songs about the coming savior. They hoped for only one or two new toys, and expected presents that were necessary like a new coat or socks. Today, we are bombarded with the many opportunities for shopping, deals, and presents. Groeschel encourages us to have a more penitential Advent season in which we really prepare in our internal, spiritual life for the coming of our Lord and Savior. We should look as the children back in Fr. Groeschel's grammar school days did for opportunities to serve and give to the poor. Fr. Groeschel describes his ideal (and usual) Christmas: he spends all day handing out food to the poor and giving out just a few gifts to the volunteers. At the end of the day he is tired from his hard work and indulges in but one simple thing – a small glass of sherry. It is the only treat he allows himself and he wishes himself a Merry Christmas. It is the service of others that is how Advent and Christmas should be defined, not by shopping malls and commercialism. This message is true for every day as well and was one Fr. Benedict often spoke. He knew that there was a need for greater substance in our faith lives lest we all lose our sense of fidelity to the Church and Her teachings.

Carrying on, Fr. Benedict also considered the bridge formed between science and faith and how it affected this greater sense of devotion to the Church. He states that it is reasonable and good when one looks for the qualities of God (one, true, good, beautiful) among nature. Science has none of this in its current form. William of Ockham used this kind of study to introduce the idea of arbitrariness, that is, that God decided that one thing was good, another evil. Luther took this and ran it into

Theology and introduced the idea of predestination (one human is destined for hell, another for heaven). While this was supposed to be a kind of reform, it really introduced a flaw into Theology. This example of "reform" is a prime example of how, through the ages, voices for change have gotten it wrong.

Voices like St. Catherine of Sienna and the many reforms that occurred with religious orders like the Cistercians are examples of those that got it right. Throughout the history of the Church and society we have had examples of those who have reformed authentically and those who have brought about inauthentic or incorrect reform. Fr. Groeschel had studied these movements enough to know that according to cyclical trends, we today are due for an authentic reform. His hope for a counter movement towards orthodoxy was fortified by this knowledge and his experience of the youth who tended towards orthodoxy[20]. Colleen Carrol's *The New Believers* was mentioned specifically by Fr. Benedict and speaks about the new young people "looking for a more fervent, authentic and honest Christianity". It is a strange time in our modern faith, Catholic education is in shambles (especially with the institutions of higher education) and the religious life is diminishing. Now is indeed the time that we desperately need reform. There are many who visit Catholic shrines like that of the Shrine of the Most Blessed Sacrament in Alabama, or who listen to EWTN that are not even Catholic. People are thirsty for faith in general and Fr. Groeschel saw this.

"I see and believe with all my heart that this Church is the historical reality that our blessed savior sent into the world to bring his word. He never told anybody to write anything down; it was the decision of the followers to write it down... He left the sacraments... several are so clear I don't see how anyone could avoid them... the Church constantly needs reform; all churches need reform. The Catholic Church especially needs reform. Why? Because to whom much has been given, much is expected."

Reformers like Saint Mother Theresa, M.C. and Fr. Benedict Groeschel and his order pushed for the need for evangelization and conversion. All faiths are in need of renewal. This renewal needs the form of evangelization, of going out into the world and making its presence know, if it is to really be effective. Fr. Groeschel did this through his many outreach programs and called the rest of the Church to do so as well.

The apostles failed and were human, so we too are failing. Fr. Groeschel respected the faith of Protestants and their beliefs as well as that of other religions, but it all of it ultimately is the faith of humans. He apologized to the Protestants for us Catholics not doing the best that we could. He was still immensely hopeful that we shared one Savior and one God and that this would someday bring us together if not in this life, the next. Eventually, Fr. Groeschel hoped that the religions would join in a united front against atheism and secularism for the good of the current culture.

It is no surprise for most of us to hear that the Church is not perfect and has not actually done this. Fr. Groeschel knew this well and did his best to love her anyway. He writes about how to handle disappointment in Mother Church in his book, *Arise From Darkness.* Being a faithful son of the Church does not mean blindly following her every command. It does mean never giving up hope and understanding that it is a human institution. Many people become so discouraged when they are let down by the Church in some way that their gut reaction is to simply leave. We are left wondering how something that is the "mystical Body of Christ" could let us down so immensely. In an attempt to give pause to those wishing to leave or who have already abandoned the faith, Fr. Groeschel asks some fairly tough questions. The first of these is what one means by 'the Church'. We could mean a building, a local organization like the Knights of Columbus or even the whole of the institution from the top down. We could mean the clergy members, those who claims to represent the Church, or those who claim to be its members. Fr. Groeschel reminds his readers that firstly, pundits, celebrities, and politicians that claim to be members of the Church are often not. "They are exploiting the Catholic Church and are making use of the more active membership that they once had in it. By their endeavors, they are certainly attacking the Church and blaspheming both the Church and her Founder."[21]

So then one must first take this into account when claiming that they have been hurt by 'the Church'. So, if it is not the talking heads in the media that define her, what does? Fr. Benedict describes the Church as the Mystical Body of Christ and reminds his readers of Ephesians chapter five verses twenty-nine through thirty, in which it is said that no person hates his own body, but protects it, feed it, and loves it. In this way, we are able to tell who is really a member of the Mystical Body of Christ. Those who love the Church and work to protect her (even if this means instigating reform or change for the better) are those that can truly say they are Catholic. There is a spiritual element to this Body that unites those who are part of it on Earth and those who are in Heaven and the blood of it is the grace that God Himself gives us.

Now, with a working definition of what exactly 'the Church' is, it is possible to move on. So, when another person says that they have left the Catholic Church for this reason or another, we must ask another set of questions, namely, "what part" or "who in particular". For it is often the case that the former Catholic or angry Catholic is upset with just a small fraction or particular sect of the religion as a whole. As a true and faithful son of the Church, Fr. Benedict Groeschel brought this awareness to those he counseled, including the religious. Those who love the Church and give much of their life in service to her are often those who hurt the worst. Fr. Groeschel writes, "Almost every priest or religious can say the [Church has failed them in some way] and has some legitimate complaint or peeve that has happened in his life of service to the Church – some place where he was dropped out or overlooked or cashiered or not understood."[22] Fr. Benedict has his own fair share of these feelings as well. He was not immune to them. He writes that it is hard to separate the people of the Church from Christ. While one understands that was not Christ that slighted them, the feelings that their Lord was somehow involved are often hard to separate or get over, even when one can view the problem objectively. Fr. Benedict invokes the beliefs and feelings of the faithful expressed in the Bible, saying that "they know that God did not do this, but emotionally they feel that they have been rejected. One hears echoes of such feelings in the words of the prophets against the Hebrews, in the writings of Paul and John."[23]

While it is difficult, we must strive to separate Church leaders and members from what the Mystical Body of Christ is. God does not fail us. People fail us. It is crucial to believe this in order to prevent becoming angry with God and possibly abandoning our beliefs in general. The Church fails us because it is made up of human beings, each tainted with Original Sin. Now, there are plenty of aspects that are untouched by this. The sacraments, the Bible both Old and New Testaments, the apostolic teachings and everything else that was guided by the Holy Spirit are included in this.

It is important to also recognize that many others have felt the same way: abandoned and hurt by an institution that they loved. Fr. Benedict, as mentioned before, is one of these people. He also mentions many saints that have been similarly mistreated by Mother Church. Padre Pio was essentially under arrest, unable to celebrate mass for the public for many years at the behest of the Pope. The well-known friend of Fr. Groeschel and his fellow Capuchin brother Solanus Casey was not allowed to hear confession and only preached once or twice for he was though too ignorant to effectively do either by higher up members of his order. St. Joan of Arc was burned at the stake by Church decree as well as derided and so many others were similarly wronged. Fr. Benedict tells a fascinating story about Bishop Bonaventure Brodrick of New York worth bearing repeating.

"Bishop Brodrick earned his living most of his life by running a gasoline station upstate. Until we had these super new gas stations, there used to be a funny little gadget on the end of the pump nozzle that caused it to stop automatically when the tank was full. That gadget was invented and patented by Bishop Bonaventure Brodrick. He lived partially on the income from it...When the United States took over Cuba...it was decided that and American Priest, Father Brodrick, would be auxiliary bishop of Havana. Bishop Brodrick went down to Cuba and, and shortly after that the Cubans decided they didn't want an American bishop. He was sent back to New York, but no one needed an auxiliary bishop. So, the archdiocese had to find him a job. He was put in charge of the annual Peter's pence collection for the Holy See. But no one wanted a bishop in charge, so he lost that job. After a long wait he wrote a letter suggesting that it might be scandalous for a bishop to be without work. The answer came back, 'Wait'. And so, he waited. To support himself, he finally opened up a gasoline station." Some thirty years later, Archbishop Spellman sought out Bishop Brodrick at this gas station where he had disappeared. He had waited thirty years for someone of the Church to find work for him, and Archbishop Spellman made him auxiliary bishop of New York.

Now, while most all of us can say that the Church has let us down in some way or another, few of us can say that the Church has let us down as badly as this. None of us have been condemned to execution by the Church, nor have we been neglected for decades. When we feel like we are so let down that we are tempted to give up, the examples that Fr. Groeschel gave us in his writing are a wonderful meditation on patience, humility, perseverance, and dedication.

Fr. Benedict also reminds us that feelings of abandonment and hurt are normal. "The problem is that when representatives of the Church hurt me, I had the same angry reaction as a person who feels that God has failed them. It happens to us all." Perhaps we hold members, authorities, and representatives of the Church to a higher standard and this also increases the degree of pain. However, the thoughtful Catholic must be mindful of the human element and be willing to forgive as God does. When we become judgmental, it is good to remember that even the apostles of Christ abandoned him on Holy Thursday and that the world as a whole is "a bit messed up". With our numbers in the billions, it is no wonder that some of those people do bad things to others; yet many are capable of and continue to do wonderfully great things, too.

As a faithful son of the Church, Fr. Groeschel wanted to preserve her and prevent members from becoming discouraged with her and possibly abandoning their faith. So, what is one to do? Fr. Groeschel says that first, one must calm down.

Secondly, one must look at one's expectations of the *flawed, human* members of the Church and see if they were realistic. Next, one must look at one's expectations of the Church in general and see if they are legitimate hopes. Lastly, Fr. Groeschel warns, one must make sure that they are not wholly dependent on the Church. While she is an amazing institution and one capable of great things, the Church is no substitution for God. Depending wholly on her will always lead to disappointment, as she is a flawed, broken, human institution. Only God is worth of our complete devotion and we must depend on Him.

Another and very profoundly deep way that so many lose faith in God is when they encounter death. Now, this is a delicate subject, but one worth looking into, as Fr. Groeschel often spoke of, wrote, and dealt with this issue. At the risk of misinterpretation, he will be quoted:

> Make up your mind to use death as we are supposed to. It can lift our eyes to eternity. And when it's a painful death, a death that may make you angry, that seems unjust and unfair- for example, an innocent person killed by malice – it is most important to pray. Then we need to remind ourselves that this innocent one has walked down a very short corridor into the light of God. However painful their dying may be, no matter how racked their bodies are with pain, the dying pass along a very short corridor. If they are prepared, they enter immediately into eternal life. We pray for loved ones on their journey that they may already be at peace with God. And we are even told by Blessed Sister Faustina, the mystic of Divine Mercy, that she believed that Christ Himself comes and calls on that soul. I believe this. Christ did not die on the cross, He did not endure what He endured in life, for people to be lost. If I were on my way to being lost, could I look into the merciful eyes of Christ and say, 'no'? The answer is I can't save myself, but I must give consent to my salvation. How God call forth this consent is something very mysterious.[24]

A good son wants all of his siblings to respect and love their mother. Fr. Groeschel did amazing work in so many different areas in terms of keeping people on the true path and preventing them from losing faith. It is in this work that he showed true fidelity to the Church. It is one thing to love your Church. It is a sure sign that one believes in an institution when one champions the cause and rallies others in support of it as well.

The title of "faithful son of the Church" encompasses so much of who Fr. Groeschel was and what he preached to his viewers, readers, and all the faithful. He was known to defend Mother Church against some of the most brutal attacks she has seen in quite some time. He was vocal against the opposition she faced by media sources such as the *New York Times* and other biased (and blasphemous) publications. He recognized that many of these sources were targeting Catholicism in general, and not just merely Christianity. He was never afraid to speak his mind on such matters, however. Quite often, Fr. Groeschel received the brunt of what critics had to say against the Church because he was so outspoken in his defense of her. He was willing to defend her position from the secular barrage of "garbage" as he called it in a true, martyr-like fashion. He was never one to do this in a self-righteous or uncharitable kind of way, however. He approached delicate issues like same-sex marriage and abortion with a caring and sensitivity that made what some think is a hard-line stance much more charitable, yet he never compromised on what the Church taught and held true to his more orthodox point of view. He was always open to a polite discussion of the matters and always made "love thy neighbor" the central focus of any discussion. He also had a deep understanding of the Church's faults and when these needed to be corrected. Fr. Groeschel realized that it was a human and therefore flawed institution and was thus one that needed reform and change in order to be better. He worked to make this a reality by founding the Order of Renewal and remaining faithful to this vision. Fr. Groeschel was also a person that had a great love and admiration for the Holy Father. He spoke highly of Pope John Paul II as well and Pope Benedict XVI and was the first to applaud their strengths as well as voice a critique when he felt the Holy Father could do more.

Fr Groeschel was also a very intelligent man. He knew so much about Church history, the lives of the Saints, world history in general, psychology, and so much more. He uniquely stood out in his love for the Church because of this. He was able to integrate all of these different areas of knowledge into a comprehensive picture of Mother Church and what exactly her purpose was, as well as the purpose of the faithful. Fr. Groeschel was able to put together how a specific type of prayer affected the psyche of an individual and how it might better their faith life. Because of this, he was not alone in his love of the Church. He was able to bring this love and knowledge to many so that they, too, shared in his sentiment and were able to grow in their own personal faith lives. In summary, Fr. Groeschel always struck a balance between fidelity to the Catholic Church and a realistic view of her faults and in doing so, stood out as one who truly knew and loved her.

Loving Father of the Poor

St. Francis spoke, "Love the poor and your life will be filled with sunlight and you will not be afraid at the hour of death." If this quote has any truth to it, Fr. Benedict Groeschel is a prime example of it. While he never actively sought death, he dismissed the ideas of participating in life-lengthening exercises like jogging or drinking beet juice. He scoffed at those that clung to life and was more than ready and prepared (and was downright excited) about getting into Purgatory. He had no fear of death and seemed actually disappointed when he did not pass away after his car accident. He knew, though, that God required more service from him.

In his book, *Arise from Darkness*, Fr. Groeschel speaks about the many different ways that people can lose their faith. Drawing from his psychological background, he is able to explain, as the books tagline says, "what to do when life doesn't make sense". He addresses in particular how the loss of security, namely, financial security, is a cause for great distress or the loss of one's faith in God. He begins his discussion by stating a well-known but little considered fact about Jesus Christ: he had very little or no security, stability, possessions, or wealth. He was always in a state of poverty and depended solely on divine help and the generosity of others for survival. He also spoke out frequently against those that were wealthy, encouraging them to give it up and dissuaded them from taking away any feelings of security based on their wealth. Many of his parables were based on this concept, like that found in Luke chapter twelve about the wealthy farmer who finally felt able secure and able to enjoy life because he had built new barns and finally had enough wealth saved. Fr. Groeschel retells the parable and then states, "This parable, like many others, does nothing to enhance a sense of security based on wealth. The message of Christ's parables and His life is this: if you are trying to make sense out of life, it is important to decide that worldly or material security is an illusion. Decide today that if you are seeking security and a perfectly safe situation in this life, you are pursuing something that is in itself very insecure – even unreal."[25] This phenomenon seems to be a problem in particular for Americans. Because of our fortunate economic situation as compared to other countries, we are left feeling that it is our right or that we are somehow entitled to security in this sense. With this being said, however, Fr. Groeschel mentions that the United States is no longer as prosperous as it once was. United States Dollars do not go as far abroad as they once did. Yet, Most Americans are unprepared to face hard financial times, except for those few, of course, who remember the horrifying times of the Great Depression. Fr. Groeschel was well aware of the many challenges that come with economic insecurity. His work with the poor exposed him to numerous accounts of those who thought they had "paid their dues" or invested enough time with a company to feel that they were secure or that they would never be put in the position to have to look for another job again. So many of us feel completely bereft of any hope when our possessions are ripped away or economic hardship befalls us. We think that as Americans we are somehow exempt from this. So, when such a catastrophe hits, a crisis of faith is often not far behind. Fr. Benedict wrote eloquently of how one should handle such a situation, saying:

"The obvious answer is Christ's teaching not to put your trust in possessions. It is not wrong to feel a little more comfortable when we are more secure than we were. That's fine. I suppose the Christ Child may have felt a little safer and sound when Joseph and Mary got back to their home in Nazareth after Herod was dead. It is by no means wrong to enjoy a bit a security and peace of mind, but don't put your ultimate trust in anything that passes away. Don't be surprised when your earthly security is threatened, because it is really always tenuous, but we simply don't realize it. Since security in this world is called into question every day, by illness, mishap, and accident, what then should we do? We need to follow the example of Christ and trust in God alone."[26]

In his work serving the poor, Fr. Groeschel was no stranger in dealing with helping people with problems of this nature. One of the critical points he makes is that we should remember that not all is lost if we remain true to Christ, but the way might still not be easy. God will not make our problems go away or reinstill us with that same former false tense of peace and security. We will not get everything back just by trusting in God. The point Fr. Groeschel makes is that clinging to God ensures that whatever happens, He will bring good out of a possibly devastating situation. With the example of the martyrs of Kyoto and Nagasaki Japan in the sixteenth century, Fr. Groeschel reminds his readers that at the point of absolutely extreme terror and pain, these people "did not expect to be delivered from physical death. They did not expect the sky to open and an angel to come down and remove them from the cross. No, they expected to pass from this world into eternal life."[27] By interacting with those in extreme hardship, Fr. Groeschel had a firsthand account of the effects that devastating economic and other outside circumstances can have on an individual and their faith life. Using his acumen form his background in psychology as well as his deep understanding of Church beliefs and practices, he was able to keep many people from abandoning God and the faith in general completely. Working with the poor means so much more than simply providing them with shelter, feeding them, or giving them adequate clothing to face the elements outside. When a person goes through this kind of struggle, it is not uncommon that they become bitter, atheistic, violent, or unstable. Because of his knowledge of Psychology, Fr. Groeschel was able to bring solace and comfort to an otherwise inconsolable group. HE was able to offer the light and hope of Christ and the Church without giving the homeless and impoverished any false sense of hope or security. Rather, he was able to give many of them the tools to cope and grow from their challenges.

Oftentimes, the disadvantaged were in this situation because of unfair employers, layoffs, or other such wickedness. Fr. Groeschel mentions this wickedness in his discussion of what to do when our security is threatened. Often, we become angry or hurt and this prevents us from making positive steps towards rehabilitation or reestablishing ourselves. We are reminded that, in the end, God's justice reigns supreme. Even when perpetrators are not forced to pay for crimes here on Earth, God will be the ultimate Judge. There are wicked people in this world. We are not all nice, kind, and lovely. God will balance the scales. Fr. Groeschel writes, "We needed the glorious resurrection of our Lord Jesus Christ so that we would know that the wicked do not succeed, so that we would know enough not to place our trust in the power of this world...Jesus Christ as an infant, as a child had people plotting against his life. You might say that he spent his whole life as a fugitive and almost never knew the kind of security that most of us enjoy. But he was given victory over all evil."[28]

Now, as someone who is destitute, poor, forgotten, homeless, abandoned, cold, or anything else of this sort, is this now a profoundly striking and comforting thought? A man who shared a similar lifestyle and was constantly persecuted, spat on, and dismissed eventually became the Savior of the world. This is truly a humbling thought and proof that God chooses the lowliest of us to work through. God can bring good out of evil. The Resurrection of Christ is proof of this. Fr. Groeschel was able to show the homeless and poor that he worked with this reality. He did not always need to resort to outright preaching or even words in general. By dedicating himself to their aid he showed them Christ's love and humility, and, ultimately, gave them hope.

One of the most striking instances in which Fr. Groeschel spoke of the poor was in relation to a talk on contemplative prayer. For those who are unfamiliar with this form of prayer, it is a rather rare thing to be able to achieve. Contemplative prayer usually occurs with very holy people and only infrequently at that. It does not come to those who seek it and is usually just a twinkling, short experience. Several saints have accounts of reaching real contemplative prayer but they are usually brief. Augustine describes it as a single instance where we see the endless stretch of eternity and God's infinite mercy and wisdom. It is brought about by a great spiritual life and does not show preference for position; cardinals or popes are not any more likely to have this experience than the poor or uneducated.

Fr. Groeschel gives the account of a young man from a devout farming family two centuries ago. He wished to be a priest or monk in his home country of France. He wanted to be a Trappist monk but was unsuccessful. All he wanted was to do this. He had the education but could not make it. So, he went to the monastery of the Seven Fountains and suffered a great depression for some time. As the darkness grew, he left for a town of Parav-le-monial where a nun had had a vision of the sacred heart. It was already a popular place for pilgrimage. "Sacred heart of Jesus, I place my trust in you" he said in commitment to Christ here. After this he travelled to Italy to enter a monastery but was not successful here either so he lived a life a travel, going from shrine to shrine. To most he looked like a mere homeless man. He spent a great many hours in prayer and shared his meager portions with the other homeless. Our Lady of the Mountain was where he finally collapsed during holy week. He died and news of a saint passing reached the people who came and flocked. The first protestant minister to be ordained Catholic in the US, John Thayer, saw his body and was instantly converted. This man was Benedict Joseph Labre. "How blessed are the poor in spirit". Upon beatification, Pope Benedict asked that the faithful admire him, but not to imitate him. God choses the poor and the weak to do His work; they are without rank, they are unattractive, they are not leaders. Even for the mentally ill there is the presence of God in prayer, even though the mentally ill or poor might not know it. Fr. Benedict Groeschel made it his life's work to make sure that the poor were aware of this great blessing and brought God to the humblest servants of God.

Fr. Benedict Groeschel uses the life of St. Benedict Joseph Labre frequently as an example of a unique and unpopular vocation. This man is the patron saint of the homeless, however, and Fr. Groeschel believed that this Saint is worth remembering. In his work with the poor of New York, the mentally ill, the homeless and even the deranged, Fr. Groeschel held that even they were capable of participating in this most power form of prayer – contemplative prayer. This prayer form, traditionally though to be reserved for the holiest and most humble of God's servants was gifted to these mentally ill people who lived in the streets. Groeschel emphasized that these people were sick in their minds and ill in other ways, but were still able to experience, even if just for a moment, that infinite expansion of eternity and God's never-ending wisdom and mercy. It shows just how humble Groeschel was that he spoke of the homeless and mentally ill as capable of this profundity. He knew that God used the weak as His instruments for good. He knew that it was the humblest servants that often did the best work for God. He also knew that he was no better than these poor that he helped and remained immensely full of gratitude for the opportunity to serve these men and women and to be able to bring the light of Christ into their lives. He did not give up on them and in this way, he was much like his friend and co-lover of the poor, Saint Mother Theresa.

Fr. Groeschel speaks candidly of Mother Theresa in an interview conducted by Linda Schafer. He said she did things because she genuinely believed it was the will of God. There is no place in the Gospel where Jesus says, "What do you think?" Similarly, Mother Theresa outclassed others and without fail would leave people with something to ponder, a thing which was rarely favorable. Groeschel believed that she was the prophetess of our modern age because she was substantially directed by the Holy Spirit and lead the Church to identify with a poor Christ; she led others to focus on the poor and knew she was not in the majority. She was dedicated, unusual, driven, and imperfect. Part of her work was bringing the church's awareness back towards service, especially to that of the poor, and leading the faithful towards a humbler life in the spirit of Christ. She was remarkable and devout.

Groeschel was the liaison between the Missionaries of Charity and the Archdiocese of New York. He claims that he failed this responsibility because Mother Theresa was so immensely headstrong. Archbishop Cook wanted Theresa to take over the Carmelite convent in New York. She refused the building. "It is so fancy, the poor people will be afraid to come here". She went to go see Cardinal Cook saying, "I am just a poor weak old woman and I don't want to lose the poverty of my order; I'd rather go home". Groeschel was humiliated, to which Mother Theresa replied, "cheer up, humiliation can often lead to humility".

Groeschel went to Calcutta in the early eighties to run a retreat for the sisters there and serve the poor as well. Groeschel spoke highly of her prayerfulness, absolute charity, and knowledge of how to handle difficult situations. She was greatly gifted by the Holy Spirit and Fr. Benedict realized that indeed she had the qualities and makings of a saint. He wanted to step down from the position of liaison due to his feeling of ineptitude. She asked why God wanted chose him for the priesthood. "God chose you to be a priest because He is very humble. He chooses the weakest, the poorest, the most inadequate instruments... I pray that when I go my place is taken by the most unattractive and ungifted of the sisters because then everyone will know that this was not my work, but God's work." One can see how Mother Theresa's words shaped Fr. Benedict Groeschel and his genuine humility and love of these poor. While they often were not in agreement, it is easy to see many similarities in their dedication and devotion to the poor.

In his tribute after his passing, it was his work ethic that especially stood out. He was unfailing in his work for the poor and in general[29]. It was said that he would work until exhaustion. Part of this work was the preservation of the dignity of the human person. He took are of others physically, emotionally, spiritually and was ever faithful to this goal. In a world where being a good person and secular success is measured by how quickly one acquires pleasure and possessions, Fr. Benedict stood out as a foil against this. Concerning the dignity of the human person, Fr. Groeschel was adamant. From John Paul II drawing from Genesis, Fr. Benedict Groeschel drew what it meant to be human and how God intended things to be from the beginning.

Adam gave the total gift of himself to his woman, Eve. Our world tells us that we can find meaning in our things and achievements. Pope John Paul II went back and tells us to give the total gift ourselves in order to find meaning. Fr. Groeschel calls us to do this as well. By giving the gift of our whole selves to others, especially in the service of the poor, we are contributing to our dignity as well as that of those we serve. When we lack this meaning and search for it in other, fleeting ways such as material goods or pleasures of the body, we are left incomplete. This often leads to neurosis because of this emptiness. Fr. Groeschel spoke in condemnation of our current society and how it relates to this unhappiness. The poor, he claimed, were capable of much greater happiness because they had nothing. He was remarkably impressed with their ability to let go and just depend on the providence of God. Those who had permanent rooms at his shelter, for instance, were less generous, more suspicious, and generally less open and kind than those homeless that just came off of the streets and had no idea where they would spend the night the next day. This lack of all possessions caused the poor to have to rely on providence. Groeschel found that they were a great example for those of us rooted and blinded by modern society.

We are made in the image and likeness of God to be in relation with each other, in love, open to life. When we relate to the "other" in a loving way, we are able to raise each other up. John Paul II called us to treat each person as a gift. Just as John Paul saw the beauty and goodness of each human person, Fr. Groeschel felt that a big part of the new evangelization was to hold each human person dear and preserving their dignity and humanity, just as John Paul II did. The youth responded to him because they were hungry for this connection and this authenticity. It is no new idea, however. It is the same faith shown through a new lens. The Saints knew all of this and so did the early Church.

Fr. Groeschel started the group of Friars and there were eight in the beginning to do the work of loving and taking care of the poor. The renewal of the Capuchins was something he was quite faithful to and he grew the order greatly, often depending and trusting only on the providence of God.

He started the Saint Padre Pio shelter and his mantra was "care for the poor". He did not just preach about it, though; his life's work was truly dedicated to this mission of his. He put in countless hours towards this goal. When they started their order, they were wondering if they should hold off on starting the shelter; Fr. Benedict Groeschel had none of it. He truly loved the poor, underprivileged, minorities and forgotten in society. The poor that he took care of felt loved and respected. He took the time to speak to them, gave them his time and respect, and they felt his authenticity and the love of Christ through him. He looked towards the help, the "lower class" and made them feel special and emphasized their dignity. Those who traveled with him spoke how no matter where he was, he looked for those who were overlooked. At fancy hotels, he would acknowledge the door man and the maids.

Fr. Groeschel did great work at the Saint Padre Pio Shelter for thirty years and grew the St. Anthony Shelter as well. He claimed that his time at Children's Village, which was a facility for orphans, was the happiest time of his life. He was there for over ten years. The kids he took care of grew up and now have children of their own. Many of them had kept in touch with their old chaplain and kept true to the faith and the values that Fr. Groeschel introduced them to. When one enters into the areas or communities where he had previously served, his memory is still very alive and there and so many whose lives have been touched by him. He had great love of the youth as well. He was known by many titles by he was most affectionately called "grandpa" by the young men at the St. Francis house.[30]

Additionally, Fr. Benedict was crucial in the foundation of the Good Council Homes. Girls come here who are pregnant or new mothers who have no other place to go. Chris Bell opened it to help those who were homeless and sought the help of

Fr. Groeschel. They offer help and resources to set up these women for greater success as people and as mothers. The whole depends one hundred percent on donations; Groeschel stepped up because his mission was to help the homeless and he loved children. He said there was no better way to be close to God than to be in the presence of a child. Jesus speaks of this in the New Testament, saying "Let the little children come to me", and "one must be like a child to enter into the kingdom of Christ"[31]. Good Council Homes have helped more than 6000 women since 1985. They take care of each other and are present to their emotional, physically, and spiritual needs. They offer the girls therapy, help them to get the necessary schooling and get jobs as well. They are there with other women and can get a fresh start. Many had previously been abandoned, abused, raped, and forgotten. This unique service was championed by Fr. Groeschel and he mentored Chris Bell closely throughout setting it up and running the home.[32]

Fr. Groeschel did not just tend to those who were monetarily poor. He also tended to those who were struggling within the faith. His time at Trinity Retreat House is a great example of this. Appointed by Cardinal Cooke of New York as the founding director, Groeschel mentored many priests and religious. His background in psychology and experience in counselling was immensely useful here, where many Catholics came to seek advice and spiritual renewal. Among those he spoke to were priests who were struggling with their vocation, Catholic leaders, and those suffering with depression and addiction. He also mentored Mother Agnes Mary Donovan and guided her through the undertaking of the founding of the Sisters of Life. She and so many others speak to his availability and desire to help, saying that no matter the hour, Fr. Groeschel was willing to help in any way that he could and offer guidance and a wisdom as well as a friendly ear. Mother Agnes in particular attributed the success of her order to the help and guidance of Fr. Groeschel[33].

It is clear that Fr. Groeschel was a man who loved the poor. While it is easy to love them in theory, or to pray for those in poverty, Fr. Groeschel actively sought out the areas where there was extreme need and poverty, where people were mentally ill, unwashed, unstable, and unpredictable. Instead of shying away from these people, Fr. Groeschel brake away from an order he cared about deeply so that he could better focus on what he through was more important – the forgotten of society.[34] When given an opportunity to help the homeless, he admitted that it cut "straight to the heart" with him. Fr. Groeschel gave everything he had every day to them. It is exemplified in his description of his usual (and also his ideal) Christmas. He serves the poor all day and takes a small glass of sherry for himself- that is all. Those who knew him spoke frequently of his exhaustive work ethic. The talked about how he would work until he was spent, giving all of his time, energy, and self in service of the neglected of our society. It is no wonder that he and Mother Teresa would have been in frequent contact with each other. Though they argued frequently, they were both strong willed and determined that all that could be done for the poor was done. It is clear that while they may have disagreed on the methods and approached their service from opposite sides, both individuals were wholly dedicated to the loving service of the poor.

As a side note, it might be argued that Fr. Groeschel also was a caretaker of those who were poor in spirit. This oft-misunderstood phrase means that one is in need of God, emptied of self and recognizes one's complete dependence on God for all graces. One who understands that life is a blessing and that it can end at any moment is well on their way to a rich spiritual life. In his work with the mentally ill, Fr. Groeschel was a true shepherd to those who perhaps clung too tenuously to life and considered or perhaps attempted suicide. For those who had a healthy poverty of spirit, Fr. Groeschel had an abundance of advice and wisdom to share with those faithful, too.

Fr. Groeschel knew that helping the poor, the overlooked, the sick, the needy, and the forgotten was crucial to the nourishment of one's soul. He spent most of his time in the service of these people. He was the first one to help when it came to the homeless and he was always willing to give of his time and talents in order to help. He founded several places of shelter in New York and other areas and was critical in helping others in similar projects. He was always drawing from the good example of the saints, both of the past and his contemporaries, as they had led the way as an example of what loving service to the poor truly meant. Those like Saint Mother Theresa and Saint Padre Pio were a constant source of inspiration for Fr. Groeschel.

Through his work with psychology Fr. Groeschel also took care of the poor in a different kind of way. There are times when those who are overlooked are not the homeless in the streets but those with no spiritual home. Priests, even, can suffer from feeling abandoned by the Church or God. Fr. Groeschel worked with many young men who were considering abandoning their vocation after being involved in some scandal or grave sin. They were hurt and sad, mentally unfit and often beaten down and hurt even more by their peers, friends, or others around them in their lives. Fr. Groeschel was able to work with many of these men and help them see what good could come out of their sad situations and what could be done to amend their ways and move on. Now, he in no way supported their past mistakes. Rather, he attempted to show them just how infinite God's love and forgiveness really is. Fr. Groeschel was able to do this for the laity as well. He was never one to deny someone based on their societal limitations. He believed that even the mentally ill were capable of a very fruitful and deep spiritual life and looked to them as an example, even. All in all, he was a man that emptied himself of self and gave it in the service of others, whether they were directly poor (i.e. the homeless, the impoverished, and the hungry), spiritually homeless and feeling bereft of faith, or poor in spirit, humble servants who looked to him as another great example of how to live a holier life. In the spirit of Fr. Groeschel and his love of language and poetry, this piece is an excellent example of Fr. Groeschel's service to others:

> If thou couldst empty all thyself of self,
> Like to a shell dishabited,
> Then might He find thee on the Ocean shelf,
> And say — "This is not dead," —
> And fill thee with Himself instead.

> But thou art all replete with very thou,

And hast such shrewd activity,

That, when He comes, He says — "This is enow

Unto itself — 'Twere better let it be:

It is so small and full, there is no room for Me.[35]

One of the more profound ways that sets Fr. Groeschel apart from others who look after the homeless and hungry is how often he uses them as a constructive example. Just as his confreres stated in a video about the Friars of Renewal, there is so much that one can learn from interaction with the poor. They are not only often some of the most generous, but also the most loving and trusting of God. Because they have often had to rely on God as their only source of anything, they are aware that God's providence is enough. They are often able to live day by day in complete trust that God will provide. Fr. Groeschel also notices that because they have often lived subsisting of so little, the homeless frequently do not share in our same fears of loss. Being used to suffering and lacking the comforts so many of us enjoy, they poor have a unique perspective. This suffering can result in the lowering of one's defenses. Instead of giving the usual response of "I'm fine", those who have experience this type of suffering are able to be honest. They will admit that they are in pain, hurting or dying, suffering or unhappy. They have no need to keep up a façade nor do they have to pretend to be anything that they are not. The suburban way of glossing over all of one's problems or feelings is so different. Fr. Groeschel mentions that those people in suburbia have too much at stake and too much to lose. They fear for their reputation, or the loss of their possessions or even their friends and family. They fear the loss of their comfort. Those who have never really had the luxury of comfort really have no fear of losing that. There is nothing to lose and everything to gain from being honest and open. It is by sharing these things that bring people closer together and really allows us to be able to give to others what they need. Fr. Groeschel wrote in *Arise From Darkness*, "We are afraid to share our sufferings. We might recall that our Lord Jesus Christ was not afraid to share his sufferings. He still shares them. That's what the crucifix is about."[36]

Fr. Groeschel did not serve the poor with a haughty attitude. He did not do it out of guilt for having so much privilege. He did not do it just because he wanted to give back or because he felt that it was the right thing to do. Fr. Groeschel worked with the poor and sought to connect with them on a real and personal level. He tried to learn from them whenever he could and he looked at each one as he would Christ. The poor, the wanderers – these people emulated the life of Christ so much better than we who have beds and a place to go each night. Fr. Groeschel saw their potential for a real and deep faith life, one that was capable of a deepness that those who have never been through such hardship would never really understand.

In so many ways it seems that Fr. Groeschel related to the people of the streets better than others. He was a unique individual who had a large and generous heart despite his tough New Jersey exterior. It was this large heart that enabled him to view the services that he did for the poor not as work but as a joyful lesson. He did everything with the mind of "what can I learn from these people" and was never one to ever dismiss someone outright because of their background, income level, ethnicity, or religion. He was an equal-opportunity servant of God and his memory and legacy are truly remarkable examples of how we, too, should act and think when we are in positions helping others. Pride never entered into the picture when Fr. Groeschel was serving the poor. He was the humblest of servants and arguably at his best when operating in this role.

Fr. Groeschel ends his chapter about loss of security with a wonderful prayer. By getting into the mindset of one who is homeless any by putting ourselves in their shoes, we, too, can grow spiritually. Let us follow the example of Fr. Groeschel and look to the poor to show us how to totally rely on the grace of God for all things, that we may be wholly trusting in Him and Divine providence. The lessons Fr. Groeschel shares from his experiences working with the poor are truly some of the most inspiring for those who suffer from fear or loss and general complacence with living a lukewarm life in both our faith and works. Fr. Groeschel writes:

O God our Father, you give us each day our daily bread. You give us what we need and often much more than what we need. You tell us in the words of your Divine Son to trust in you and to rely on you for all things. Often, we are filled with fear. We are afraid to lose our security, our place in life, our health, our reputation, what we style as our importance. We are afraid to live and more afraid to die. Give us your Holy Spirit that we may find our peace in you. Strengthen us in hours of need. Most of all, may your Holy Spirit teach us to see what is truly important and to surrender that which is really unimportant and perhaps an obstacle in our road to you. May our Lord Jesus Christ, the poor carpenter of Nazareth, the homeless preacher of the roads, the man condemned to death and deprived of all earthly things, including this life, be our model. May we not wish to be more secure than He was. And when things are taken from us and our security fails, may his example and life be a guiding light to us through the short journey of this life. Heavenly Father, you alone have riches to give that time cannot carry away. You alone can give us that Kingdom which does not parish. We pray, O Lord, that through the example of your Son and the grace of your Holy Spirit, we and all of those dear to us may have a true security based on the acceptance of your Divine Will. May we have eyes to see beyond this world and hearts to cherish that which does not pass away, but which lasts forever. Amen.

Ardent Preacher of the Gospel

It is commonly known that Fr. Groeschel was an amazing orator and preacher. He did so not only from the pulpit, but on the street, through his writing, and through his television presence on EWTN. He was extremely knowledgeable about the Church, its history, and so many other aspects like psychology that he was able to integrate into an approachable, humorous, and intellectually edifying message. He was also very human and so aware of the suffering of the human condition. His fatherly demeanor was able to inspire and touch so many. While it may seem that some of these qualities do not relate to his preaching of the Gospel, Fr. Groeschel had the uncanny ability to preach the Gospel through his loving actions and hard work.

He also speaks so fondly of the saints. He showed great respect for those who lived out the ways of the Gospel. He prays always with God's mercy at the forefront. He constantly roots his opinions on the Scriptures as well. Considering this example of Divine Mercy, Groeschel talks about how justice is the flipside of mercy. He uses the Ten Commandments as an example of justice, but reminds us that the Psalms are just as important because they mention and remind us of God's divine and infinite mercy. Fr. Groeschel continually speaks about the Beatitudes also. He describes their importance, especially those about mercy and the poor.

In his prolific writings, Groeschel is habitually quoting scripture and referencing those Saints that lived according to the words of the Bible. Even in just the introduction of his great work, *I Am With You Always: A Study of the History and Meaning of Personal Devotion to Jesus Christ for Catholic, Orthodox, and Protestant Christians*, there are five Scriptural references within the first three pages. To be an ardent preacher of the Gospel, one must in fact know the Gospel well. It is clear that Fr. Groeschel was highly schooled in the scriptural traditions and defended them and the truth of the Church passionately.

A great example of this is his vehement opposition to the Historical Critical method of Scriptural interpretation. He believed that the modern tendencies towards "spirituality" and the less credible forms of "New Age" beliefs as well as the abandonment of religion were the result of this mode of thinking. These superstitions bubble up when there is a lack of any real faith. There is a human need for the divine and the religious. When real religion is not present, the human heart searches it out in other and incorrect places. It ultimately is a violation of the first commandment.

In his talk about the devotion of Christ, Fr. Benedict Groeschel speaks rather candidly about his condemnation of the Historical Critical Method of Scripture interpretation. He traces it back to the Rationalists and how they dismiss the miraculous. It is because of the Scriptural miracles like the multiplication of the loaves and the fishes, however, that we humans are able to accept Christ's divinity. God gave us these miracles so that we could believe. Just because one cannot prove the miracles does not mean that they did not occur. After all, none of us were there (so said the Jewish neighbor of Fr. Groeschel). Father had the benefit of being a doctor of psychology and a man well versed in the scientific method. He often pointed out that the first rule of science is to avoid proving a negative hypothesis, or, that something did not or could not occur.

In addition, Groeschel goes on to poke several other holes in the Historical Critical methodology. The members of the Jesus Seminar (the group of men that got together and formulated and expounded upon this method) are constantly revising their methods. If they were sound methods of investigation and yielded correct and valid results, there would be no need for the constant updating. Even at the onset, most of these methods were intellectually refutable. Additionally, their aim to reconstruct the real, historical figure of Christ is invalid from the start. No historical figure can truly be reconstructed in such a way that we in the present are aware of what they thought, felt, or intended. One of the largest problems with the Historical Critical model is that the historical picture really has very little to do with reality. We cannot even get inside the mind of someone who died twenty years ago, let alone two thousand.

Fr. Groeschel asks that even if we were to believe what these men in the Jesus Seminar are saying, why would we give up the whole of our faith on the basis of what seventy so men are preaching? It is the job of the Church to remind us that Christ is with us in a very real and present way. We are not to abandon the truth of our faith, nor are we to dismiss the miracles because they do not fit into a tidy picture of Christ that someone else is trying to paint. To dismiss the miracles of Christ is to discredit the Holy Scriptures. While it was not the idea of Christ to write them down, but that of His followers, they are still inspired and guided by the Holy Spirit are not to be tampered with. The deism of the early history of America is seeping its way back into our faith and is a very dangerous heresy[37]. This again refers back to the causes of unbelief; intellectuals that believe in their own mind more that God are arrogant and usually fall away from the faith. The human mind is simply not capable of understanding everything.

Fr. Groeschel writes about how this flawed cultural backdrop is part of why we need spiritual renewal and reawakening in his book "The Reform of Renewal". He writes:

"During the past twenty-five years, which have been a period of relative economic prosperity and upward mobility for most members of the Church in Western countries, there has been a gradual loss of the sense of reform and repentance. This has come about partly because of the declining awareness of the conflict between time and eternity, between earthly contentment and eternal happiness. This decline is so enormous that for a Christian writer to suggest that we are choosing the wrong side of the conflict or that a conflict exists is practically scandalous. To question whether our values are too humanistic is to suggest that we have lost a prophetic element in our Christianity. To raise an outcry against the worldliness and moral flabbiness of contemporary Christians is to risk being dismissed out of hand...but that does not remove the need for reform – either personal or ecclesiastical."[38]

This culture has made it easy for the Gospel to get distorted by men like those of the Jesus Seminar. Even within the faith there has been need for renewal and Fr. Benedict Groeschel was not one to shy away from the facts, however harsh they may be. He wanted to set the stage for a better, strong Church so that the attacks from the outside on the Scriptures might be better fought.

Fr. Benedict Groeschel was not just a defender of the Gospel, though. He was able in his sermons, speeches, and writings to make the Gospel real and present to those who heard him. Groeschel made Jesus human without taking away any of His divinity. Fr. Benedict did so with his uncanny ability to bring the scriptures alive to his audience. In his book, "Tears of God", readers are immediately faced with a powerful quote from Anne Morrow Lindbergh, saying that tragedy "is buried and overlaid with new life…the long road of insight, suffering, healing, and rebirth is best illustrated in the Christian religion by the suffering, death, and resurrection of Christ." Fr. Benedict Groeschel springboards off of this concept and this is how he gets his title, "Tears of God". For the Christian person encountering this work, the tears of God are the tears of Jesus of Nazareth, the man who suffered a horrific death and encountered much hardships and opposition in his short time here on Earth. In his writing, Fr. Benedict Groeschel was able to communicate the spiritual truth that were especially pertinent or helpful to his readers all while tracing these ideas back to the heart of our faith, Christ Jesus. His preaching was not merely a call to imitate Christ as one would in His time, but in ours. The aforementioned book basically outlines how one can deal with catastrophe or great tragedy in one's life and in the loves of those they are very close to. One of the saddest repercussions of tragedy is the loss of faith in the Church or in God completely. Fr. Groeschel tells us a story about a family that was decimated by robbers, leaving but one parent alive. He prayed for these people and felt the grief of the situation; he calls for us to meditate on these tragedies and to remember that we are not exempt from them in our lives. It is wise to reflect and to think how we would react to such situations. He does not say that anger at God or cynicism is an incorrect response, however. Taking from the words of Jesus, who even asked God why He abandoned His son, Groeschel reminds us that is how we deal with this response and how we allow God to bring goodness through it that defines us. He states that we can look at the suffering of Christ, His followers, and the whole of the Early Church to come to understand just how God uses catastrophe as a part of the greater work of the big picture of Salvation, both for the individual and the whole of the human race. In this way, pulling from the divinity and humanity of Jesus Christ, Groeschel makes a marvelous outline on how we humans are to handle some of life most perilous problems. The Scriptures become not just a didactic Sunday school tool for lessons, but an honest, useful application for us to get past hardship and to let it be a way that we grow deeper in our faith and love relationship with God[39].

He was not one to merely accept the Catholic teachings of Catholicism at the exclusion of all other faiths, however. Fr. Groeschel was appreciative and supportive of many other faiths including Judaism, Protestantism, and the Orthodox faiths. While he of course held that the Roman Catholic held the fullness of truth, he looks towards the other faith as a point of comparison and spoke often of the many great similarities that were shared between them and us Catholics. In his book "I Am With You Always: A Study of the History and Meaning of Personal Devotion to Jesus Christ for Catholic, Orthodox and Protestant Christians", Groeschel breaks open the Gospel to include these other believers and expounds on just how our means of devotion to Christ are similar. For instance, he speaks of how each of those faiths mentioned in the title believes that Christ is somehow still with us. We all demand that the response to this presence of God be love, even though each of us expresses this love quite differently. Pulling always from the Scriptures and his knowledge of them, Groeschel comes up with this amazing definition of what devotion really is to these faiths, saying that it must include (1) powerful psychological awareness of the personal presence of Christ and a strong desire in the human person for this presence of Christ (2) an appeal to Christ about personally important things in one's own day to day life so that this devotion is able to become a real relationship and not mere meditation or contemplation (3) a willingness to do what God asks of us, which includes the scriptural elements of forgiving others, loving, and praying for our enemies (4) being full of repentance, as all Christians call for (5) trust in Christ and God's plan for us, offering our petitions with confidence that He hears and answers them (6)the eschatological fact that one is indeed mortal and that while the end of time is not a t the forefront of their thoughts, their devotion is sustained by the hope that God will accept them into His bosom at the end of their life. Over and over, Fr. Benedict reminded his audiences that devotion was the key to interfaith dialogue. He goes on to reiterate what Pope Benedict XVI had said about the devotion, namely, that by encouraging it and studying Jesus we are able to begin to understand Him better and this in turn helps us with our personal relationship with Jesus Christ. We are able to have a more real and intimate connection when devotion is part of our spiritual life. Fr. Groeschel notes that devotion was largely on the decline during the difficult time of the seventies and eighties, when revolutions of all sort were occurring and sexual permissiveness began to seep into the culture. This then allowed room for an increase in mere talk and intellectual study of Jesus and this really became the primary way Jesus was talked about and studied. This "historical Jesus" was chosen over the one we worshipped. Instead of debating over which prayers were best suited for adoration, people sat and discussed whether he was more of a reformer, revolutionary, or simply a preacher. This changed the whole climate concerning the person of Jesus. The historical facts gathered about Him are rather unimpressive. Doubt is encouraged about His divinity because none of it can be proved beyond a shadow of a doubt. Then again, very little of His life can be proved. What one is left with, then, is a shadow of a man hardly deserving of a second thought, let alone adoration and praise. Fr. Groeschel writes:

"What did Christ think? Some fundamentalists are quick to say he knew everything they know, and in the same way that they know it. Some of them think that the infant Christ spoke Hebrew perfectly. The rationalist smugly asserts that this is obscurantists thinking, and not borne out by the Scriptures as we read them today from our informed modern perspective. But the rationalist cannot be sure of what Christ knew. Therefore, in a magnificent burst of illogic known as reductionism, he decides that Christ, the God-man, knew nothing. Rationalists often seem to describe Christ as being in a state of divine retardation."[40]

It is easy to look at orders such as the Jesuits and hold them partly to blame for this emphasis on the intellectual. They are by no means the enemy here, however. Fr. Benedict Groeschel was one to point out that the Capuchins have a slightly greater emphasis on feeling and the Jesuits, thinking. However, one can see in his interviews with those like Fr. Joe Castielle that this difference was largely complementary. The Jesuits believe in the importance of adoration and devotion, but emphasize that there must be truth behind it or else it is not authentic. The Capuchins, historically not as well educated as the Jesuits, though were still intelligent. This did (and still does) color their types of devotion. This variety, however, offers a great deal of beauty to the faith. With this said, it was no secret that Fr. Benedict was rather disappointed with many of the Jesuit universities concerning their authenticity of faith and devotion. He credits the renewal of the order to Pope Saint John Paul II and Pope Emeritus Benedict XVI and say hope for the future of Catholic Universities.[41]

In his exploration of the person of Christ in this book, "I Am With You Always", Groeschel is quite different form the men of the Jesus seminar why implement the Historical Critical method of Scriptural interpretation. He accepts His miracles as well as the message of Christ. Jesus of Nazareth, to Groeschel, stands alone because he was one of the few in history who was able to do God's will, call others to find out God's will in their lives and to answer life's great questions by seeking God in a wholly non-violent way. The human condition is not an especially happy one all of the time but God has offered us an answer to this desperate and suffering state that we are in with the words of the Our Father, "Thy kingdom come, *Thy will be done*".[42]

In his efforts for reform, Fr. Benedict again preached the Gospel through his actions and uses the Gospels as a means of guiding his renewal efforts. He writes in his book, "The Reform of Renewal":

"It should come as no surprise that constant repentance, the regretful acknowledgement of sin, is one of two essential components of the Christian life. It is also clear that reform, the positive effort to change and overcome our tendency toward evil, is the cutting edge of an integrated Christian life. Those who pretend that the community of followers of Christ is perfect have neglected to take into account this important fact of life. Christ never claimed that His followers would be perfect, that is, beyond repentance and reform. The vacillating fisherman, whom Christ chose to be leader of His community, is a compelling example of this. The Gospels recount Peter's constant falls and temptations, and Tradition suggests that his wavering continued too the end of his life. Awareness of the need for reform is simply the reflection of the conflict between time and eternity, between the self-seeking and self-transcendental…"[43]

As stated previously, Fr. Groeschel was a prolific and gifted writer. It is arguable that Fr. Groeschel's best preaching of the Gospel was done through his many and varied works. Part of what make them so amazing is their depth as well as their adherence to the Gospel truths. Fr. Groeschel was able to bring those truths into the modern world and put them into a light that makes them relevant for the modern reader. Instead of coming across as preachy or boring, Fr. Groeschel always managed to remain interesting and lively, even while addressing serious and important topics. Additionally, he wove the Gospel into his writing gracefully. At times it is almost imperceptible, his use of the Gospel. He was often very subtle and employed his vast knowledge in a way that completely avoided the off putting "Bible thumping" kind of Scriptural writing. Additionally, much of his writing was not focused solely on the Gospels. Rather, he chose other subjects such as psychology and history and reinforced his message with use of the Scriptures. It fortified and supported all of his work, both written and oral. His points are not simply Bible verses, but well thought out arguments peppered with complimentary quotes and (most importantly) explanations of what they mean and exactly how they are relevant.

In a discussion on whether the results of sin could be good, Fr. Benedict reminds us of his great love for beautiful language. Like, poetry, Song of Songs reminds us, "Love is as strong as death…its flashes are flashes of fire, a most vehement flame. Many waters cannot quench love, neither floods can drown it (Song 8:6-7)." In this way, Fr. Benedict reassures his readers that love is a force powerful enough to overcome sin. In his own words, "Good results [of sin] always require that the sin be the occasion for some greater love, one that brings repentance and redemption… we know that love overcomes sin in our own lives.[44]" With the beautiful quote from Song of Songs, Fr. Groeschel brought light into this discussion of sin, offering hope to the sinners, which is really the whole of the point that he is trying to make. Further on, Fr. Groeschel reminds of the Sermon on the

Mount and the challenges that Jesus tasks His true followers with. This is the point at which Christians are called to love unconditionally and give themselves up. It is a sermon on actively loving one another, not merely refraining from breaking God's commands. It calls of action, not inaction. Now, Fr. Groeschel explains, "The Sermon on the Mount calls us to difficult and painful abnegations, but it also calls us to a love that goes beyond sin and just desserts to the works of love. And love, as the singing poet John Denver has pointed out, is 'like the ocean, full of conflict, full of pain'"[45]. Note, it is rare that a preacher of the Gospel is able to weave together modern culture, the Scriptures, the message of Christ, and their own points together in such a way. Fr. Groeschel is willing to draw from these other sources for inspiration and interest without cheapening his message and while staying true to the Gospel truths. In just a few pages later in his book, Fr. Groeschel speaks about the need for the Christian to be well-integrated to achieve the status of "blessed" that Christ speaks about on the Sermon on the Mount. One must be consistent while also adhering to the rather controversial values and lifestyle that Christ gave us - the very lifestyle and values that eventually lead to his execution! Even when the path is not easy nor the ending necessarily a happy one, Fr. Groeschel holds true to the teachings of the Gospel and never stops encouraging his audience and all of the faith to remain true to them. He goes on to say that a well-meaning Christian, if left unintegrated, is a poor example of the Gospel. One who is integrated incorrectly by accepting false teachings or the incorrect values is a detriment in that they are no longer just a poor example of the Gospel, but are capable of actively leading others away from the Truth. Those who are in leadership positions, Fr. Groeschel warns, should keep in mind the warning that St. Paul gives in his first letter to the Corinthians, namely, that the caretakers of the Church need to be trustworthy. A great preacher of the Gospel must know how to defend it. Fr. Groeschel knew better than most the hardships of being a leader and the consequences of not leading the proper way. He also understood that the Gospel message is a challenging and unpopular one with much of modern society. Still, he embraced it and truly tried to live his life within the boundaries set by Christ and His followers.

This was not the only way that Fr. Groeschel tried to preach the Gospel through his actions and writings. Jesus did not just give His followers a list of rules for us to follow and another of goals we should strive for. Jesus' message was one that was central to who He was and how He lived His life. As Christians, we are called to follow Him by imitating His life. In a discussion on dread and its ill effects in "Stumbling Blocks or Stepping Stones", Fr. Groeschel tells his readers about the unique effects that dread can have on a person and their psyche. He discusses where it comes from, how to deal with it, and how to avoid its many damaging effects. While his primary discussion is on the psychology of dread and how it can warp the spiritual life of a person, he is able to comfort his audience with the reminder that even Christ Himself was subject to dread. In the Agony in the Garden, Jesus asked His father to spare His son from the torment and fate to come, should it be His will. Fr. Groeschel entwines this Biblical narrative into his broader discussion and in doing so helps his readers in a real and impactful way. He writes, "…It was the end of Him and His teaching, and the religion of salvation he had proclaimed. It was oblivion; his followers were filled with dread. We have seen from the account of the agony in the garden that He Himself was filled with dread. Christian tradition believes that at least symbolically He took on Himself all the dread of every child of God who ever lived. It was the dread of nothingness, emptiness, and ultimate failure that Christ accepted that night.[46]" Being reminded that their God had participated in this suffering that they, too, feel, helps the wounded person to overcome the negative effects Fr. Groeschel speaks of that come about from experiencing this emotion. In fact, sharing one's dread with another is the first thing Fr. Groeschel tell us to do when we experience it, as it lifts the burden off of us somewhat. In this Scriptural account here, Fr. Benedict gives all Christians someone to share in this suffering with them – Christ Himself. With this in mind, one is then able to use dread for the greater good of deepening one's faith. When there is nothing else left, there is God and one's salvation. Here, Fr. Groeschel brings up another vivid image straight from the gospels. It is St. Peter calling out to Christ as he slowly sinks into the Sea of Galilee. When all hope is lost, we must remember to turn to Christ.

Much of Fr. Groeschel's writings are geared towards making sure that the Cristian person is prepared for the challenges that life throws at them as they attempt to live out the gospel truth. Fr. Benedict writes, "The simplicity of the road of confidence in God is almost frightening to us. We are so complicated that we believe the secret to leading a good Christian life must be complicated too. But it as simple as the Gospel – and just as hard to follow.[47]" Fr. Groeschel was under no illusions about the challenges of living out the Gospel message and was not shy about his own struggles as well. He was also well versed in the struggles that many of the Saints had throughout history, too. The examples that Fr. Groeschel gives are meaningful and realistic; they are brought to life for the reader through his wonderful story-telling abilities and are thus more impactful. He also approaches each story with such mix of mystery and conviction that it is hard to not be drawn into his writing. For instance, Fr. Groeschel speaks of Brother Francesco Maria of Comporosso in a story considering the sin and effects of envy.[48] Fr. Groeschel places us in media res as an older brother readies himself to begin his day. This man, known among the poor and affectionately treated by them, garnered envy from the Father Guardian. While Francesco was later made a Saint, his Father Guardian was not. We are left with the moral of the story and feel as if Brother Francesco was someone we knew. His suffering and hurt were described in such a way that the reader understood the ill effects of envy, pitying the old man. Fr. Groeschel made this Saint real and exemplified exactly how envoy works its evil. Even Saints are the subject of envy by those desiring their piety. They, too, can be hurt by it. There is something very spiritual in the way Fr. Groeschel makes the Saints of old real to modern readers. We are able to connect and learn from the holy example they give as well as their flaws. These people are human. They are not passive figures in a stained-glass window. Fr. Groeschel brought the Gospel alive and showed us how to do it right by giving so many of these realistic accounts of the Saints and other holy people he had learned of or knew.

Fr. Groeschel was not one to count himself out, either. He gave his audience multiple examples of how he had made mistakes in his life path as he tried to follow the Gospel message. After trying to use his status as a priest to validate a point, he was called out by a woman who then asked why he wasn't nicer if that were the case. Dumbstruck, Fr. Groeschel asks, "Could there be selfishness and self-seeking tendencies in my attempts to be generous? Could I be giving with strings attached, with hidden agendas, with subtle expectations? Was I working for the Gospel or myself? After thirty years of religious life, was I still selfish? And, of course, the answer was yes."[49] While maintaining honesty about his own foibles, Fr, Groeschel never seems self-righteous. He is more relatable and he offers up how he was able to address and overcome his many sins in a humorous way. Fr. Groeschel preaches the Gospel dynamically. He brought the Good New to so many people and in so many ways. He was also a realistic man. He writes in his book "Stumbling Blocks or Stepping Stones", "We have to protect ourselves sometimes in order to recoup energies. It is of little use to remember that a saint would not complain under such circumstances. We are not saints, so we must have the humility to admit our limitations."[50] By the same token, though, he was always reassured by God's power. Ever a mild pessimist, Fr. Groeschel reminds his readers frequently that the life of the Gospel is not an easy one. Just a Christ was hated in His time, so His followers are in this one. Those we try to show love and forgiveness to will hate and hold grudges in return. "If you love Christ, you must walk the difficult road to Calvary. But you will begin to see yourself borne by powers that are beyond you."[51] Fr. Groeschel understood that preaching the Gospel did not mean standing at a pulpit on Sundays. He knew that it meant going out into the cold streets and giving of self in the service to the poor. He knew that it meant striving to act in a Christ-like manner. He knew that preaching the Gospel could be done anywhere, at any time, and in any media, whether that as behind a camera taping for a show on EWTN or sitting down at a desk and writing a book. He knew preach the Gospel much be engaging to the audience, and was not limited to merely the Scriptures. Fr. Groeschel was able to blend anecdotes about his life, his vast knowledge of the Saints and of history, poetry, current events and so much more into a message that always left the audience member wonder how they could do or be better; and that it truly what it means to have a love for the Gospels and to preach and follow them with conviction.

Dedicated Follower of St. Francis

The life of St. Francis is a story most of us know, but bears repeating to be shown in the light of just how exactly Fr. Groeschel was a true devotee of St. Francis. This Saint was born in 1182 to a wealthy merchant family in Assisi. He received a vision from God to repair His church. After selling off his father's goods, Francis was disowned and embraced a life of poverty and simplicity. He begged for food and cared for the poor on his way, taking care of lepers and started his mendicant order under the blessing of Pope Innocent III. Eventually the order grew to include the Poor Claire's and contemplatives and well as mendicants.

St. Francis served as an example not just for Fr. Groeschel but all Christians in general. In Fr. Benedict's writings about what occurs when a member of the faithful feels let down by the church, Fr. Groeschel hold us St. Francis as a great reminder, writing:

"Then we come to St. Francis of Assisi. We are all familiar with the happy pictures of St. Francis and the friars. To tell the truth, St. Francis lived the last years of his life pretty much in exile. He had few companions, and his order was governed by a man, Elias of Cortona, who was really his worst enemy. Elias did not even die a Franciscan. St. Francis suffered because very few people shared his vision...stuck between indulgence and arrogance, sentimentality and fanaticism, they never really understood this holy man, who saw himself as very simple. We learn not to depend too much on any particular part of the Church but to put our trust in God."[52]

Using this beloved Saint as an example, Fr. Benedict weaves realism into his writing. He is able to pull from centuries ago and make the problems and struggles of the faithful who have gone before us a reality. In many ways, Fr. Benedict's devotion to the saint makes his relationship with Francis much more like that of two good friends. There is more credibility and sincerity there. As his audience, we are left with an example that can bring real comfort and sympathy to our pains. Fr. Benedict makes St. Francis real. Along the same lines is Fr. Benedict's discussion of how we ourselves can be our greatest enemy when it comes to sin and darkness. Fr. Benedict reminds his readers that, "St. Francis made a terrible mistake in his life. He did it out of good will and naiveté. He let in every Tom Dick and Harry who came along and wanted to join his order. At the end of his life, there were five thousand men in the order, and perhaps half of them should have gone home. He let in too many men too easily. Don't think that only sinners make mistakes."[53]

What a blessing it is to truly get to meet this human being. Without the rosy lens of history to look through, we are left with a rather real and raw account of who exactly St. Francis was. It might not be the picture we had in mind of the childhood devotional cards with a cherub-cheeked man flocked by gentle woodland creatures. However, as Benedict Groeschel writes, a mature person requires a mature faith, or they will surely leave the Church. So, this rougher image we have of St. Benedict gives us a great deal more actual instruction and guidance as we navigate life's tough roads. He is human, and serves as a great example of how to weather the storm well and come out for it all the holier.

Pope Benedict is adamant that St. Francis was no nature-worshipper, but rather was so holy that he attracted living creatures and humans to him and his cause. St. Francis did the hard work of founding the order of the Franciscans. His little band of men when and changed the way that Catholics participated in their faith. God called St. Francis with the simple words of "Go, repair my church, for it is in ruins". Francis converted his live and others towards the faith. Fr. Benedict has done it in the same way, living an incredible example for others and drawing them to God with his devotion. Chesterton said of Francis that he was known as an eccentric, which Fr. Terrence Henry states might indeed also be a way that Fr. Benedict Groeschel imitates the great Saint. He also claims that Fr. Benedict has another similarity – that while he often was carried away, he also seemed to land on his feet, due to the fact that his feet were always planted firmly in Rome. Francis was looking to bring about renewal in the Catholic Church out of a genuine love for it. Heeding the call of Pope John Paul II, Fr. Groeschel followed in these footsteps of St. Francis quite literally and was able to serve the poor and make loving service more of a priority for those within the church. He reached out to the spiritual poor as well as those who had little wealth. In the United Stated we have great wealth, but many continue to starve. Those with much have little spiritually. Groeschel reached out to both. The renewal Groeschel drove and supported was one that fought both kinds of poverty. He led people to greater love, community, and healing. The culture of death continues to wear on society and individuals. Fr. Benedict was a brother to everyone and led so many greater into Christ through his ministries and tending of the poor. He embodied the spirit and work of the small man from Assisi that began the Franciscan order. True to this same spirit, he also sought to renew this order in order to remain ever faithful to the heart of what St. Francis taught. Groeschel saw the work of the Franciscan University of Steubenville, his work in the Franciscan Order of the Renewal, and the work of his confreres as the continuation of St. Francis' work and that of God. He believed that it was indeed divine providence and intercession that allows people anywhere to do God's will. Humans are imperfect and still somehow God helps up to do His will.

Groeschel was not upset that numbers in his Order of the Renewal were dwindling. He attributed this fact to the cleaning up of the religious orders. Previously they had strayed from their original messages and intents; Groeschel was happy to see that they were really turning around. Instead of being sad that this order he had started was dwindling, Fr. Benedict was hopeful, saying that he had always hoped that The Franciscans of the Renewal would be able to rejoin the Capuchins.

Fr. Benedict Groeschel started the Franciscan order with but eight other friars who shared his vision of renewing their former Capuchin order. Because reform was a term not allowed by the Holy Father, they adopted the term of renewal to distinguish their fledgling group. It attracted many men, especially young ones, who were drawn to the particular community and work of this order. Many wanted to be active in New York, where there are unique challenges particular to the area and a there is a great need for help for the poor. The founders were looking to really live out the vows of poverty chastity and obedience as outlined by St. Francis in a more profound and intentional way. So, with the approval of the Archbishop of New York, they started the Franciscan Friars of the Renewal in the South Bronx. They are very active with the youth of the area. It is said that "the Franciscan plant does well in very poor soil". In the South Bronx and Harlem, these men are able to do the most work. In the spirit of poverty as set by St. Francis, they actively seek out these "undesirable" areas to help. It is written into their order that if the areas should greatly improve, they are to move and seek again that poor soil. This said, they do not have such pride as to think that they are the ones that are bestowing the gift of faith and religion to these people; rather, one friar notes that it is often the poor that show them how to live lives faithful to Christ, for they rely directly on His providence and so very often have nothing else. In this way, the men of this order follow in Benedict Groeschel's way and the way of St. Francis[54]. It comes as no shock to most to hear that the time after the Second Vatican Council was one of upheaval, change, and uncertainty. At this point in his religious career, Fr. Groeschel was the Director of the Office of Spiritual Development for the archdiocese. He was involved in many programs that were intended to help the faithful navigate the rocky course of the times in both the Church and Society at large. It was during this time, however, that Fr. Benedict felt that many of the actions and practices of his order of the Capuchins were inauthentic and lacked the "deeper prophetic witness" he felt was necessary to be spiritually successful. When he started his order, Fr. Benedict was led by the example of Blessed Mother Theresa of Calcutta and her devotion to the poor. After seeing how young women flew to the order, he knew that there were others in the Church that wanted the same things that he did and that the youth especially were hungry for more of this brand of spiritual work. His co-founders saw this desire for renewal as an example of Fr. Groeschel's deep love of the Franciscan way of life and this effort to preserve the original intents of the founder particularly admirable. Fr. Groeschel tore out the secular ways that many orders had adopted into their life and sought to restore the core values of religious life. As Sister Lucille Cutrone said of him, "His heart was very much like St. Francis: He loved God; he loved the Church; he loved religious life, and he loved the poor."[55]

According to those who knew him at the time, Benedict Groeschel was one of the holiest seminarians. He had a burning desire to run things differently than how they were going and was so disappointed with many of the events that occurred in the late twentieth century both in the Church and in secular culture. Fr. Benedict Groeschel wanted to change this and began his reform order under the blessing of the Holy See and Father General of the Capuchins. While there were many higher up within the Capuchin order that were not thrilled with this event, they were largely respected and treated with dignity and kindness. Just as the original reformers of the Catholic faith during the time of the Reformation did not wish to start a new group, Fr. Benedict sincerely hoped that things would have improved enough within the Capuchins that his order would be able to reunite with them before his death.

The three vows that these men take are the particular and unique way that they choose to live our God's call for them. They are meek, poor in material ways, obedient to the will of God and the wishes of the order, and chaste. A young friar describes this vow not as one of deprivation of the flesh and love in some heroic feat, but a redirecting of that love to God, the one who created us and gave us that unique ability to engage in the act of love. These are the ways that Christ has called these Friars to live out their vocation. They live a life of prayer as well; it is in this way that they are able to really achieve success in following these vows. They express the love they have for God, listen for His will for them so that they may be obedient and are fortified in His graces in order to become meek and humble servants without all of the distractions that so often come with worldly life[56].

St. Francis had the vision for his order to be prayerful like monks but to be able to enter into the world as well. They are "monks of the marketplace". Fr. Groeschel made this a cornerstone of the Friars of the Renewal. They are not cloistered by any means; they are a present and real form of Christ's love for so the underprivileged in society and those communities where they are located. A New York Times video documentary does an amazing exposition of this in which the beautiful chants play in the background as the video shot shows graffiti and impoverished areas in the Bronx. It seems like a startling juxtaposition and one cannot help but wonder if St. Francis looks down and smiles about this religious center nestled amongst the very poor of New York. The gangs, the drugs, the debauchery seems like a frightening backdrop for this religious community. While many Friars expressed some initial reluctance, perhaps, at the onset of their time there, they all truly feel that there is no other place better for their service. There is so much need in this particular community for help. One Friar mentions that many shelters in New York are dangerous place; they offer safe refuge and a rare thing for these homeless- a small slice of peace and security in a loving, familial environment[57].

Fr. Benedict Groeschel's great love of St. Francis was also colored by his background in Psychology. Father was very interested in the Saint's great love and reverence for Christ, which ultimately led St. Francis to spread the devotions of the Eucharist to many people. St. Francis was also enamored by the presence of Christ and popularized the prayer forms of the Christmas Crèche or the Nativity Scene as well as what later developed into the popular devotion of the Stations of the Cross. He also was one of the first to encourage reverence for the Blessed Sacrament outside of the liturgy and strove to make it a universal practice among believers. More in the psychological realm, however, St. Francis had an extremely psychological response to his love of Christ, as manifested in his having the stigmata. St. Francis is also believed to have visited the holy places in Palestine and his devotion was so strong that the friars have taken care of these sited since then.

He also, much as Fr. Benedict did, encourage a real and genuine spirituality based on the Bible and the love and admiration of the words of the Gospel in particular.[58]

Fr. Benedict Groeschel writes in his book "The Reform of Renewal":

"We live in times that desperately need reform and spiritual renewal. I believe that this call to the revitalization prompted by divine grace is beginning to grow. I find it eagerly accepted by a growing number of young Christian adults. In the readjustments being made in response to the new role of women there are much bitterness and pain, but not so much among the young…"[59]

Fr. Benedict Groeschel's devotion to the Franciscan order expanded to include all of religious life. While he worked to reform his own Capuchin order, he did much to help in the renewal of religious life in general. In his book, "A Drama of Reform", Fr. Benedict writes:

"This way of life [religious life], which has taken many forms and produced many saints and good works since the third century, is today in desperate condition in much of the world. Religious communities, which are required by their public commitment to follow their rule and constitutions, are dying out in many places, including America, Europe, and European-style countries such as Australia. The average age of most members is well above sixty, while there are few or no recruits. Just a half century ago, in the years after World War II, religious life was flourishing, with thousands of new members each year and impressive works of charity and faith. The discipline of religious life was somewhat oppressive and at times a bit inhuman. Members themselves were very sincere, with a high degree of dedication to God and the need of the human race. Today, Catholic religious life is flourishing in Latin America, Asia, and Africa, while is appears to be dying in northern Europe and the English-speaking world. What is much worse, it is not dying a holy death. Despite the presence of large numbers of older religious men and women who often yearn for the spirituality and obedience that they knew when they entered the life, some religious communities are filled with dissent from official Church teaching and the norms of Sacred Scripture.[60]"

Just as Fr. Groeschel was dedicated to his order and way of life within the Franciscan worldview, so was he devoted to the person of St. Francis and all of the other saints. He had a great deal of respect for these "friends of God", as stated before, and he was always looking to them as an example of how to live one's life in a holy and meaningful way. When in doubt, Fr. Groeschel always looked to the saints for inspiration. His devotion and affection for Mother Theresa is a very clear example of these. Even though he admits to frequently disagreeing with her, Fr. Groeschel speaks of her with the highest level of respect and admiration. Her holiness was apparent and her conviction that she was doing the will of God was a quality that Groeschel often mentions and praises.

Though he worked with and knew Mother Theresa on a personal level, she was by no means his only saintly friend. Padre Pio was one of those whom Fr. Groeschel also greatly admired and spoke of on many occasions. On an Episode of Sunday Night Live, Fr. Groeschel goes deeply in depth into the life, work, and admirable qualities of this saint. A stigmatic following on the same path as St. Francis himself, St. Padre Pio was a Capuchin as well. A devoted man of the Franciscan way of life and all that came with it, Pio was admirable for his strong desire to follow in the footstep of Christ and to participate in His sufferings. He offered up his own suffering to the cross and was blessed with the stigmata. He bore the wounds of Christ quietly and modestly, though, and did his best to not attract attention to this miracle. This humility was indicative of his great holiness, devotion to St. Francis and the religious life in general[61]. Fr. Benedict does mention that there have been nay-sayers and those who have denied the miracle of St. Padre Pio's wounds. These people, however, are in direct denial of the Scriptures. While skepticism has surrounded the wounds of this holy man, the denial of the miraculous directly contradicts the Scriptural assertion that God does perform miracles. In this way, Fr. Benedict continued his work as a great defender of the Gospels.

Though the stigmata is arguably St. Padre Pio's most famous miracle, many others are attributed to him as well. For instance, though he never left his small village for the last years of his life, he was reported to have been in other places around the word and bi-located. Vana Litzani was a young girl who experienced this. Seeking to make a confession, she entered her church and the janitor told her that no priest was there. Despite this, she thought she saw a priest enter and so she went in the other side to make her confession. Years later, she would meet Padre Pio and recognize him as the man that had heard her confession all those years ago in her youth. There are many other accounts of similar stories, as well as those of other miracles. For instance, he was also known for digging into the minds of those who gave confession to him, often asking, "Is that all?", and sensing when there were omissions or falsehoods within a confession. He was also prophetic to many, stating their call to the vocation before they had even converted to the faith or other aspects of their lives. He also could sense when there were unholy people about him, calling them out as "bad and sinful" people and seeing into their heart of hearts.

Like all miracles, God gives us these instances so that we can better believe in Him and His saving power. Though they are a reminder of God's greatness, they are also indicative of the holiness of St. Padre Pio. The saints struggled a great deal with the same human flaws as the rest of Christianity, sometimes even more so. God uses people, especially those who are lowly and humble, to bring about His will and goodness into the world. It is no surprise that God would choose Padre Pio as his servant, being a poor and simple peasant from a small, rural area. These miracles serve as a reminder that God is real and present in our lives and that we are all capable of doing God's will and living holy lives.

It is true, sadly, that these chosen ones of God are often hated by society and are persecuted for their beliefs and holiness. St. Padre Pio was a man that, just like St. Francis, wished to be holy. Unfortunately, this simple goal left him vulnerable to attack. It is true, though, that Jesus warns His followers of this in the Scriptures. What is harder to imagine is that there are still those even within the faith that are unwilling to admit the miraculous events of Padre Pio's life. While many of the skeptics come from the outside and fuel their skepticism with the general suspicion of the Catholic Church, those within the faith are just as troubling. Pope John Paul II was not one of these people. Despite those that claimed Padre Pio's miracles were falsified, Pope John Paul II took the man, his life, and his miracles quite seriously. Having visited Padre Pio early on in his priestly life, Pope John Paul was the major proponent behind his beatification[62].

There are so many ways by which Fr. Groeschel was able to show that he was a dedicated follower of St. Francis. In a broader sense, he was a champion of all saints and was able to make so many people realize that these is so much spiritual richness to be found by considering these people as one's friends. This kind of relationship with the saints gives the faithful a new outlook on these holy people and gives realistic and wonderful examples of how to live one's life as well as the types of spiritual goals that we should be setting. In a more specific sense, it is clear that Fr. Groeschel was dedicated to St. Francis through his devotion to his order. As a true Franciscan, he saw the need for reform and undertook the hard battle to start the Order of Renewal, despite the hardships and the negative input of many of his former Capuchin confreres. Though doing so was arguably the harder road, he was not afraid to take it. In his heart, Fr. Groeschel felt that to remain true to the original principles of St. Francis it was necessary to do so. It is often much more of a struggle to stand up to those we love than it is to stand up to these we perceive as our opposition or our enemies. Fr. Groeschel did this out of his desire to follow what he believed the heart of St. Francis' preaching and work was. Additionally, he lived his life in a manner that imitated the life of the great saint. He lived in poverty, spent most of his life helping the poor and the forgotten of society, and he preached against the more secular ways of the church. He did not cave into the pressures to accept the status quo and adopt the ways of the world. Just like Francis he thirsted for a more authentic way to practice one's faith. Just like St. Francis, Fr. Benedict also had an overwhelming love for the Mother Church. He loved his faith and did what was necessary to preserve orthodoxy and authenticity within her.

In Conclusion

The four categories that we have looked at had been thoroughly explored. Indeed, Fr. Benedict Groeschel was a faithful son of the Church, loving father of the poor, ardent preacher of the Gospel, and dedicated servant of St. Francis. In so many ways he touched lives and brought the light of Christ to some of the darkest places. His mild pessimism kept him from seeming to holier-than-thou, and he was approachable. The mentally ill came to him for help, the poor asked him for food, the homeless asked for shelter, the lost asked him for guidance, and so many others came to him with their needs. In all of the research conducted for this summary of his life, not one instance was found where Fr. Benedict asked something of others. He was careful not to burden others with his presence, and even joked in his old age that he was lacking in use. This could not have been further from the truth. He was a man full of spiritual insight, wisdom, and much grace up until the very end of his life. He gave so much of himself up for the service of others and worked so hard throughout his life, even to the point of exhaustion, that his time in Purgatory will surely be short, if he undergoes any at all. This man was a fearless leader. Headstrong and caring, he forged the way for so many other lives and cleared the path towards God and the Church for even more.

Fr. Groeschel quite clearly made a huge impact on the world and those lives that he touched. It is hard to say that this writer knows the man Fr. Groeschel. Just as he even criticized those who supported the Historical Critical method of Biblical scholarship, it is foolish to think that one can reconstruct a whole person. While I do not propose to do so, this writer feels the need to express a heartfelt love for this man. It was not necessary to ever shake his hand, hear him in person, or be touched or helped by him in any direct way to gain this admiration. Simply with his writings, his presence on EWTN archives, and personal accounts of him, I was completely and utterly changed. We are all often faced with spiritual darkness and just as the Capuchins required a renewal, so do our own souls. The darkness of doubt, of that lack of hope, and of uncertainty has been lifted by this project. Bubbling forth with a new spiritual zeal, I often found it hard to continue writing. Inspired, the desk was often left so that soup kitchens could gain another volunteer, or mass could be heard, or a friend could be visited in prison. It is difficult to see how the love of the poor, of the Church, of the Gospel, and of St. Francis contributed to the holiness and peace of Fr. Benedict Groeschel and not follow in his footsteps. It is so easy to become complacent in our lives or our faith. Faith should never be easy. It should challenge you, bring you out of yourself and open your heart in love of others and Christ. Fr. Benedict of all people recognized this and knew it. He embraced hard work and setbacks, made the most out of failure and hardships, and knew that sometimes all you can do is laugh at life's absurdity.

The setbacks of life are so hard to handle and deal with. It is all too easy to become discouraged and disheartened when things do not meet our expectations. Fr. Groeschel joked about being a mild pessimist. He states that he felt bad for his optimist friends, claiming that so often they were disappointed by things in life. He and other mild pessimists, however, were not disappointed. Like other New Yorkers (mild pessimists in their own right), he expected the worst and when it did not happen, he was overjoyed. Now, while not everyone is built this way, participating in the joyous acts of love that Fr. Groeschel did does make for a much happier life.

Bubbling with the knowledge and love of a new friend, friends and family were regaled with all of these facts. While it would not be fit to call it a miracle, the miraculous shows itself in different ways. Blessed by the presence of the Holy Spirit and inspired by the life and works of Fr. Groeschel, this writer found a new, renewed love of the Faith, the Mother Church, and Jesus Christ. As Fr. Groeschel often said, the Saints are the friends of God. I could not help but feel his blessing as I asked for guidance through the course of this project; it was the presence of a true friend of God that inspired, enlightened, and loved.

Let us pray for the man we so recently lost, who many will never get the privilege to meet. For those who have, may you remember him well and speak often of his great works, seeking to imitate his love of the Church and the poor, his steadfast and encouraging preaching of the Gospel and his dedication to the great

St. Francis. Let us pray for the repose of his soul and a safe and quick journey through the Purgatory that he so looked forward to.

Prayer for the Departing Soul

O Lord Jesus Christ, You said through the mouth of the prophet, "I have loved you with an everlasting love: therefore in my pity have I drawn you to Myself." Deign, I implore you, to offer up and how to God, the Father almighty, on behalf of your servant, Fr. Benedict Groeschel, that love of Yours which drew you down from heaven to earth to endure all Your bitter sufferings. Deliver him from all the pain and sufferings which he fears that he deserves for his sins, and grant salvation to his soul in this hour when it takes its departure. Open to him the gates of life, and cause him to rejoice with Your saints in everlasting glory. And do You, most loving Lord Jesus Christ, who redeemed us by your most precious blood, take pity on the soul of Your servant Fr. Benedict Groeschel, and lead him into the lovely places of paradise that are forever green so that he may live with you and from those whom You Chose. You who with the father and the Holy Spirit live and reign, God, forever and ever. Amen.[63] –The Roman Ritual

[1] Fr. Benedict Groeschel would say on many different occasions that while he tentatively considered other careers, he did not seriously consider any vocation except that of the priesthood or religious life.

[2] Where, he would ironically note, he was treated with much greater respect as a religious than at some of the Jesuit and other Catholic colleges throughout the United States.

[3] Apostolate for Family Consecration. "Episode X." *Sunday Night Prime.* EWTN. Irondale AL, Television. https://www.youtube.com/watch?v=CrVebIHQ0Io

[4] N.B. all Biblical quotations are taken from the New American Bible unless otherwise noted

[5] Apostolate for Family Consecration. "Episode X." *Sunday Night Prime.* EWTN. Irondale AL, Television. https://www.youtube.com/watch?v=CrVebIHQ0Io (emphasis added)

[6] "Jesus of Nazareth". *Sunday Night Live.* EWTN. Irondale AL, Television.

[7] "The Jesus Seminar was a group of about 150 critical scholars and laymen founded in 1085 by Robert Funk under the auspices of the Westar Institute. The seminar active in the 1980's and 1990's. It preceded the short-lived Jesus Project, which was active 2008 to 2009 (Wikipedia)." John Dominic Crossan is a noted member. These scholars use the historical critical method of approaching Jesus of Nazareth in their search for the most historically accurate depiction one can find of Him. As a result, they dismiss the miracles, resurrection, and much of the Gospel accounts of Him. They were a particular thorny subject with Fr. Groeschel.

[8] "Jesus of Nazareth". Sunday Night Live. EWTN. Irondale AL, Television.

[9] Prayer of Praise and Thanksgiving

[10] Stumbling Blocks or Stepping Stones p.3

[11] ibid 14

[12] Stumbling Blocks or Stepping Stones p19

[13] Mother Theresa

[14] The Coming Home Network International. "Authentic vs. Inauthentic Renewal" https://www.youtube.com/watch?v=uUCiHmD1l9k

[15] Fr. Benedict Groeschel, Stumbling *Block or Stepping Stones* p.37. The latter mentioned here is problematic because they do a great deal of harm. When they speak of their faith and have an infantile depiction of God or the beliefs of the Catholic Church, they misrepresent the faith as a whole and are at fault for these inaccuracies.

[16] Stumbling Blocks or Stepping Stones, p 39

[17] Ibid p 40

[18] Ibid p43

[19] Ibid p 53

[20] For example, the proponents of abortion said that the youth would be on board with the change and that the opposition would eventually die away. Yet, it is the youth that are really leading the anti-abortion movement and pushing for change.

[21] Arise From Darkness P. 62-63

[22] Ibid p. 65

[23] Ibid

[24] Ibid p. 123-124

[25] Arise from Darkness p 44

[26] Ibid p. 47

[27] Ibid p. 48

[28] Ibid p. 50

[29] Sunday Night Prime – A tribute to Fr. Benedict Groeschel https://www.youtube.com/watch?v=KTGIKa5BbrI

[30] Ibid.

[31] Fr. Benedict on Good Council Homes https://www.youtube.com/watch?v=YzFDhqaznnE

[32] Good Council Homes https://www.youtube.com/user/goodcounselhomes

[33] Fr. Benedict Groeschel: 'A Heart for the Poor' http://www.ncregister.com/daily-news/father-benedict-groeschel-a-heart-for-the-poor/

[34] In an interesting biographical note about St. Francis, the man is said to have been repulsed by society's forgotten until one day he met a "leper and gave him a coin; then, in spite of his enormous dread of leprosy, he embraced the man, desiring to love him just as Christ loves each of us (Stumbling Blocks, p. 147)."

[35] This version occurs in Madeline L'Engle's book "A Ring of Endless Light". It is usually attributed incorrectly to Sir Thomas Browne but was in fact written by Thomas Edward Brown and was first published in "Old John and Other Poems" in 1893 under the title "Indwelling".

[36] Arise From Darkness p. 28

[37] Devotion and Scripture by Fr. Benedict Groeschel https://www.youtube.com/watch?v=YGj9tNpzNNY

[38] The Reform of Renewal by Fr. Benedict Groeschel

[39] Tears of God by Fr. Benedict Groeschel

[40] Stumbling Blocks Stepping Stones p 46

[41] Sunday Night Prime Jesus of Nazareth

[42] I Am With You Always by Fr. Benedict Groeschel

[43] The Reform of Renewal by Fr. Benedict Groeschel

[44] Stumbling Blocks or Stepping Stones p 17

[45] Stumbling Block or Stepping Stones p 19

[46] Ff p 54

[47] Ff 61

[48] As further evidence that this man knew the Scriptures, Fr. Groeschel points out that envy is frequently addressed in the scriptures and reminds us that it reaches from Adam and Eve to Cain and Abel, King Saul, David and some of the Prophets, just to name a few.

[49] Stumbling Blocks or Stepping Stones p 83. He actually spells out near the end of the book that the Gospel was his source for writing. He says, "In exploring apparent psychological problems, I have tried to draw answers from the teachings of faith in the Gospel. My purpose has not been to imply that the first process was erroneous. Rather my intent has been to examine the impact of Christian revelation and personal faith on the conflicts and difficulties of life (P. 143)."

[50] Ff 84

[51] Ff 87

[52] Arise from darkness p 76

[53] Ff 98

[54] Franciscan Friars of the Renewal PART 1 https://www.youtube.com/watch?v=M35GO_RoIZo

[55] "Fr. Benedict Groeschel: 'A Heart for the Poor' http://www.ncregister.com/daily-news/father-benedict-groeschel-a-heart-for-the-poor/

[56] Franciscan Friars of the Renewal PART II https://www.youtube.com/watch?v=grpL-eeJ4Ao&spfreload=10

[57] N.Y. / Religion : Friars of the South Bronx https://www.youtube.com/watch?v=GZQcXhUqMmU&list=PL1ZdrWTOAHho0Y343AXRi3jrrAs-qZPlz&index=9

[58] I Am With You Always by Fr. Benedict Groeschel

[59] The Reform of Renewal by Benedict Groeschel pg. 1

[60] A Drama of Reform by Fr. Benedict Groeschel pg. 22

[61] Fr. Benedict was indeed a contemporary of Padre Pio and even received a mailing from him. Though they were both capuchin brothers, those in charge wished to keep hordes of people from going to visit Padre Pio so as to steer away from it becoming a spectacle.

[62] Story of Padre Pio, Sunday Night Live

[63] "Recommendations of a Departing Soul", Collectio Rituum (The Roman Ritual) (NY: Benzinger Brothers, 1964) p. 204. As found in *Arise From Darkness* p. 177

Comprehensive List of Sources
Devotion to Christ by Fr Benedict Groeschel, CFR. (n.d.). Retrieved November 1, 2014, from https://www.youtube.com/watch?v=YGj9tNpzNNY

Authentic Vs. Inauthentic Renewal. (n.d.). Retrieved November 3, 2014, from Renewal https://www.youtube.com/watch?v=uUCiHmD1l9k

Father Benedict Groeschel: 'A Heart for the Poor'. (n.d.). Retrieved November 1, 2014, from http://www.ncregister.com/daily-news/father-benedict-groeschel-a-heart-for-the-poor/

Father Benedict Groeschel: 'A Heart for the Poor'. (n.d.). Retrieved November 1, 2014, from http://www.ncregister.com/daily-news/father-benedict-groeschel-a-heart-for-the-poor/

Fr. Benedict Groeschel on Good Counsel Homes. (n.d.). Retrieved November 3, 2014, from https://www.youtube.com/watch?v=YzFDhqaznnE

Franciscan Friars of the Renewal PART 2. (n.d.). Retrieved November 1, 2014, from https://www.youtube.com/watch?v=grpL-eeJ4Ao&spfreload=10

Good Counsel Homes. (n.d.). Retrieved November 2, 2014, from https://www.youtube.com/user/goodcounselhomes

Groeschel, B. (1990). The reform of renewal. San Francisco: Ignatius Press.
Groeschel, B., & Marczuk, G. (2005). A drama of reform. San Francisco: Ignatius Press.
N.Y./Region

 Friars of the South Bronx - NYTimes.com/Video. (n.d.). Retrieved November 1, 2014, from https://www.youtube.com/watch?v=GZQcXhUqMmU&list=PL1ZdrWTOAHho0Y343AXRi3jrrAs-qZPlz&index=9

Show #120 "Death & Purgatory" Father Benedict Groeschel CFR. (n.d.). Retrieved November 1, 2014, from https://www.youtube.com/watch?v=CrVebIHQ0Io

CPSIA information can be obtained
at www.ICGtesting.com
Printed in the USA
LVHW062330080920
665395LV00020B/2607